The Holy Grail
of Our
Flat Earth

Martin Liedtke

BewleyBooks

The Holy Grail of Our Flat Earth
First published in 2019 by
© BewleyBooks.com

Cover Design by: Angie Alaya
Cover Photography by: Martin Liedtke

Digital ISBN: 978-1-909426-36-8
Paperback ISBN: 978-1-909426-38-2

PUBLISHER'S NOTE
The chapters presented in this book are transcripts from Martin Liedtke's YouTube
channel. For the titles to each chapter, please see the references in the Appendix
section of the book.
Please also note that a publisher's role is to remain impartial and may not necessarily
agree with an author's views, descriptions or observations or uphold all of the content
explored. However, BewleyBooks works on the premise that all avenues of education
should be sought and explored, and the reader should be able to learn whatever
interests them and, from that learning, make their own informed decisions along their
life's journey.

www.BewleyBooks.com

DEDICATION

I would like to dedicate this book to Maureen, my wife, and
Carole, my mother. Both clocked out last year.

ABOUT THE BOOK

All the research in this book revolves around proof that the earth is flat. The evidence you will find within these pages is based upon books from ancient history and photographs from our recent past.

In *The Holy Grail of Our Flat Earth* Martin Liedtke has woven together so many important pieces of information on energy, weapons, war, art, culture, politics, and environment that it's almost impossible to disagree with his findings. Amazingly, few people are covering human history in the same way.

The opening chapter alone reveals the richness of Martin Liedtke's findings. Here, in his first book, you'll begin to understand the secrets that have been hidden from humanity and, more importantly, Martin's work encourages you to start to question; why?

The Holy Grail of Our Flat Earth presents transcripts from a man who should be classed as a legendary archaeologist. He's a forward-thinking speaker and mentor, and with this book, Martin aims to bring his most popular work, insightful knowledge, and intensive research to a much bigger audience in a simple and straightforward language that anyone can pick up, read and understand.

With *The Holy Grail of Our Flat Earth,* you will become aware of Martin's enthusiasm as he teaches lessons and presents nuggets of wisdom on the real history of the world. You will marvel at his fact-filled and fun way of sharing his decades of insights in an easy-to-understand style. But, more importantly, you will be able to learn valuable lessons on what our ancestors have been capable of – and how we can rectify this.

Martin Liedtke goes into much depth about why we now need to become aware of what has happened and unlearn the false lessons we have been taught to believe.

PRAISE FOR MARTIN LIEDTKE

Normally when you read a book, you fall into another realm and escape from reality. In Martin Liedtke's book, however, you may begin to identify the illusionary world which readers seek to escape.

Martin's intuitive work exposes the establishment's world 'history' which forms a fictitious reality. Thankfully, Martin shows present day visual reality and then back-engineers it to show our true history.

The Holy Grail of Our Flat Earth will present you with a choice; self-wonderment or self-denial. You will find that there are three sides to a coin, contrary to establishment education.   *Febbage*

The civilization before us was wiped out by a major cataclysm as little as 200 years ago. We are the inheritors of this great advanced civilization who left their buildings, technologies, arts, and infrastructure behind. The only problem is that history left this great civilization out of the history books. Instead, we were taught lies which have finally run their course. *The Holy Grail of Our Flat Earth* exposes these lies and reveals to you the truth. *JonLevi*

Martin Liedtke is a modern-day historian, YouTube presenter, speaker of truth and a total paradigm shatterer! In his first literary offering, Martin takes us *literally*, on a major walk on the wild side.

This book is part one of the new author's work, throughout which he provides us with incontrovertible proof for our flat earth realm whilst dismantling the common historical narratives of our so-called past.

The proverbial 'wool' is about to be totally obliterated eternally, and with new eyes, the obvious, in plain sight, will once again align our senses. Be prepared, best read while seated! Buckle in!!!!   *Melanie Helen*

The Holy Grail of Our Flat Earth

Martin Liedtke

BewleyBooks

CONTENTS

ACKNOWLEDGEMENTS

This book is the result of a particular persistence to get to the truth. However, the immense task this research has thrown-up would certainly not have been possible without a group of wonderful, and equally persistent, people. If they had not taken part in contributing their findings this book wouldn't be in your hands today.

It is with gratitude I thank them for their interest, hard work and tenacity to hunt down and locate relevant documents, images and information. All this aligned with the concept that we really are living on a flat earth and their contributions have made this work possible.

Lee Mowat, Flat Earth British subscriber channel, what would I do without you Lee? Then there's Jon Venezia (Levi), who has come up trumps every time. Also, I would not have been able to do without the UAP channel - thank you so much! Alexander Mlletic from AlexOutOfMagic has been very helpful too – couldn't have done it without you.

I cannot forget Rebecca, as she does *everything* from managing my website FEBinfo to keeping in touch with all the people I don't get a chance to speak with. Thanks so much Rebecca.

And, of course, there is the great Flat Earth British (FEB) Think Tank, the wonderfully talented translation team, as well as all you people who unselfishly shared your knowledge, wisdom and insight. Thank you so much for all you've done.

Martin Liedtke, 2019

FORWARD

It's still the year 2019, or so they say. Whoever 'they' are, also often say that History repeats itself, in fact, they repeat select idioms until nobody questions the veracity of widespread notions. The greatest hoaxes are the ones done in plain sight, lasting many generations, portraying the truth in truisms while violating the veracity of it behind every little detail. If history repeats itself, is it the fake history or the real, or both?

As true accounts were unjustly relegated to the outer fringes of society, the gaps left behind were filled in with devilish prevarications. Despite consistent repetition of these fabricated stories, with precise details to underpin falsehoods, the most important truths may still exist in a certain masterpiece, somewhere. Strangely enough, it's likely to be found in the most derided sources available. First of all, if you'd ask me, it's to be found in Holy Scripture, (I speak for myself here). Additionally, writers like Martin are no strangers to public derision without investigation.

Until the recent work of researchers like Martin, and the phenomenon of YouTube (sans censorship) and the few other (struggling) successes of the modern truth movement, things were bad for a long time and getting worse. When tell-a-lie-vision PROGRAMMING ruled the air, only a precious few writers and lecturers could be found doddering about without much fanfare. With a small audience of mostly ostracized, independent, misfits of society (and science) in tow, they managed to present, preserve, and even pervade some important ideas with supporting research (both forgotten and new experiments) publicly here and there. A heroic effort that yielded only a seed crop for the next generation. The seeds were scattered in a sea of misinformation, among weeds of controlled opposition, and the burning heat of continual trolling and derision by the uninformed masses who took neither the time nor the effort to investigate the matter at hand for themselves.

Fortunately, by some unknown sea of change, the landscape is transforming for the better rapidly. While most people are not yet saying 'the earth is flat', many people are now reluctant to declare that 'it is not flat'. Many are privately questioning whether the Earth is indeed a 'globe', as they were always taught it was, that Classroom Globe except no supporting brackets, and scaled up to 40,000 km in circumference. Why? Perhaps the realization hits them that all, and I mean all, 'pictorial evidence' of the Earth as a spinning space-ball is an artistic work of one type or another. It seems logical, then, for every basic assumptive 'fact' to be verified by more reliable data, indeed anything outside of one's personal experience becomes worthy of cautious scrutiny.

Thankfully, more researchers like Martin and I share what we find, and what we think, to provide a framework for the rich sources of new information that dwarfs the feudal conjectures of 'Truther' materials of years past. It's becoming a nourishing food-for-thought that any curious mind can thrive on. No more does one's natural wonder waste away while scrounging for table scraps among scattered vestiges of truth. What is found today is still no easy task, like gems mixed in piecemeal fashion alongside cheap ornaments and decoys. Only the wise may find wisdom in fables, fairy tales, legends, Children's books, mythology, fictional works, even in the vague seeds of otherwise 'ridiculous' superstitions. Martin, like myself, and many of you, already gained sparks of inspiration, and a sense of some kind of deeper truths in such materials as these, despite this inhospitable environment.

At every turn, the high priests of our reality hid evidence, destroyed the treasures of our past, squelched real education as rumours, denounced independent thinkers as paranoid conspiratorial ne'er-do-wells, all while holding a monopoly on the narrative. It's time for new narratives to challenge the status quo. The way Martin does this is unassuming, favouring inspiration of the type that a friendly neighbour would offer (if you were ever fortunate enough to have one of these) over the imposition of a strict authoritarian teacher (that, unfortunately, I'm sure you have experienced more than once).

The answers are coming, and hopefully, if History repeats itself, the knowledge gained will usher in a new golden age before any dystopian reset is heralded by strange booms and blasts of 'trumpets'. Whatever has been devastating regions all over Earth, however it originates, "let us form a better resonant frequency, one of peace and joy for the benefit of all Mankind", I say, being only one Underrated Actual Physicist, a name conferred to me by some of my subscribers. I know Martin agrees, and that makes two. What about you?

Onwards and upwards!

UAP, September 2019

PREFACE

Stop anyone from coming to their own conclusions about the shared history of humanity, and you end-up alienating them or putting inside them the urge to figure it all out for themselves. This idea is particularly true of Martin Liedtke, avid researcher, tireless educator and now, author of all the findings he has unearthed with the help of what has been termed the 'hive mind' – like-minded people with a need to reveal the truth.

Martin quickly realised that the idea of proving this is a flat earth plane, gathering all the information needed, was too broad a subject for himself to tackle alone. For this reason, he began a research process that started online, on YouTube. With it, he invited people from all over the world to send him their questions, ideas and evidence so that he could gather them together and give a clear presentation of the truth.

Through his online appearances, Martin has reached a wider audience than he ever hoped possible. With his no-nonsense approach to library records, historical tomes, and remarkable photographs and illustrations, he has been able to give clarity to what a lot of people would consider a mind-bending topic.

As soon as his audience began to grow, Martin knew he was onto something important but, like all people who begin to impart their knowledge, his humble heart was unclear where it would all lead. A revelatory programme of events followed hot on the heels of his introductory expositions. Clues left for archaeologists to dig up are rare, but Martin has found enough of them to understand something was hidden from humanity that needed to be exposed and told.

People like Martin Liedtke make you believe this earth is a magical place. It makes you think that, even with all the problems, the horrors, and the misery that we witness around the world every day, anything is possible.

As with the tales of myths and legends, through an interest in unearthing the truth about our world, Martin has dug up the real history of humanity and, if you're not prepared, it can take you somewhat by surprise. His revelations stimulate your imagination and, if you are determined enough, you too can begin to put some of the puzzle pieces together. Martin actively encourages you to.

Books available today have made it all the easier to find out what has happened. I say easier, not easy. Because, while the clues are there, a considerable amount of effort has been made to conceal the order of events. Why? Who knows why? I only know that I'm excited by what Martin's curious mind has found out. The research he has managed to take the time to do, with the miraculous assistance of many good people, about this earth we live upon is the stuff of legends and the heroes who have fought to preserve it.

The excitement Martin must feel at being at the cusp of this new view of humanity's history must be easier to imagine than to explain. It doesn't take much determination to dig up the story of humanity, but it does need boundless enthusiasm – and Martin has this in abundance.

Some may not now, or may never, take any of what he reveals in this book, seriously. But you can't deny, it makes for a profoundly fascinating conversation. What he has found out, lets us know that there is more to this earth than we have been led to believe. Even if you cannot comprehend what he is about to tell you, just by his revelations here, there will be something inside you that begins to question all you've ever been told.

Our earth is real enough. We live and breathe it every day. To those who are new to this type of 'alternative-history' research, you may approach the contents of this book with a curious mind and perhaps may even feel a little threatened by it. For, you must ask, if certain people in powerful positions can easily create a false narrative for the masses, then the question must be asked, what else are they capable of? Fortunately, this is not my story to tell. Revealing the true history of our world and this earth we live on, is Martin's path in life.

Next time, when you look around you, at the hills and the dales of your country, you could be forgiven for thinking that's all there is to it. Just a landscape to breathe in and admire. The lush green land, the tall waving trees, and the sparkling blue sea, ice still lakes, and cool rushing rivers – all could fool you into believing you are living in a kind of paradise. But, just a scratch at the surface, a little dig at a curious dent in the landscape, and the earth gives up her secrets - for those who are prepared to think for themselves.

The Climate Change scenarios that abound around us may drive some people to the edge of the thought that 'The End is Nigh' and encourage them to wonder where's the point in it if we're all about to die in ways beyond our control anyway? But Martin, through his passion for the truth, encourages all of us to not accept things at face value. To question all we are told and to seek the answers that our intuition urges us to enquire after. And, perhaps, even begin to change the system itself.

If you are not inspired by the questions that history raises, you will accept what you've been taught by rote in school. But, if you trust that niggle in your gut, turn your eye to see something else, something that you've always accepted as fact, and begin to question its real purpose, that's when the truth is revealed.

Martin's book attempts to raise those questions and answer them. He begins to tell the story of humanity's history, backed with archaeological evidence, statistical data, facts and figures that are easily found in ancient books written by people who were there at the 'reset', people with enough of a conscience to leave clues for their children to find.

Martin's book gives you an idea of the vastness of his research and at his tenacity to get to the truth. He doesn't only mention one source, but hundreds. Literally. This should give you an idea that some of this is real, based on fact and should get you to question what we have been taught and, more importantly, why.

Martin's work is a revelatory guide to what we haven't been told about our past. His interpretation of events and the reasons for them are fascinating to even the most innocent ear. He strives for the truth as he sifts through the research that has been gathered and, unlike many educators, Martin is happy to explore the answers with you.

Kaye Bewley, BewleyBooks.com

INTRODUCTION

The Holy Grail of Our Flat Earth brings together information from every available source to show you a history we have been actively discouraged from finding out about. It gives you insights into what happened to our ancestors, and why. It shows you that Technasma and humanity go hand-in-hand and that many people over the years have sacrificed their lives to get this information to you.

In *The Holy Grail of Our Flat Earth*, I present these chapters that walk you slowly, step-by-step, through what at first seems like an impossible reality. With the information brought together in this book, you will get an overview of how much is not real and what is.

You can look at the photographs in the book and check them out on my YouTube channel where you can take part in this fascinating adventure. As well as this, my book aims to serve as an introduction to you, bringing to you the reality of humanity's existence.

Each chapter links to another and introduces the methods, timelines, architecture, and weapons that were used to get us to the life we see before us today. To help clear up the mystery of what is the globe/flat earth argument, each chapter will give you an example from factual evidence.

I do have to put a disclaimer in here though as it is

important to make sure you understand I know the information given here is not a guarantee of facts as they were experienced at the time. Those generations have gone and no one is alive today who experienced it first-hand. All we can rely on is the official documents and photographic evidence left for us by them, then piece them together to figure out what was real.

The Holy Grail of Our Flat Earth goes into some detail about how this re-set system works, to help you understand what has happened and what is happening. I will try to make it as comprehensive and yet, straight-forward, as possible so that you can see for yourself the clues that have been left.

The information in this book is not meant to scare you, rather, it is meant to encourage you. From this, you can start to notice what is going on and, more importantly, what has been going on, throughout the history of humanity. How our ancestors have coped with it and recovered from it, is a subject for another book.

The objective of *The Holy Gail of Our Flat Earth* is to provide you with an outline and to give you an overview of the reality of the situation around you.

The Holy Grail of Our Flat Earth can help you with your questions. It might not give you all the answers, but this book can be used as a tool when you talk to other people, people who haven't had their eyes opened to the possibilities of our infinite existence and the power that humans have.

To understand better what is presented in this book, I have divided it into the topics as follows:

- The Reset System
- Technasma Devices
- Fasces - the Emblem for Fascism
- The Flower of Life
- Magnetism
- The Vortex and the Cross
- The Holy Grail
- The Axis Mundi

I've also included a chapter on the secrets of Amsterdam. These topics, when brought together, show you how our current world and perceptions of it, were created. It also points towards two inevitable facts:

1. that this plane we live on can only be a flat one

2. which can only mean that there is a Creator

Each of the following sections is presented in no particular order but, it would be difficult to understand the flat earth scenario without bringing them all together. For example, it makes no sense that previous generations were far advanced in their use of weapon systems if you don't understand how those weapons worked and what results they brought about. It would also be difficult to understand how humanity today is unable to use free energy without the knowledge of Aquatec devices used by the Romans (or Phoenicians).

The reasons that are often given to us as an explanation for all the catastrophes throughout history are that they were:

- electrical discharge events
- giant stones falling from the sky

- brimstone and thunderbolts
- plagues and pestilence

It is a well-documented fact that as a comet passes overhead, mental illness and hallucinations are caused. States of mental health are altered, where people get confused about what's going on. The question to ask is, not what causes these emotional disturbances but, instead, what causes the sky to go black like a nuclear winter? In truth, a massive volcanic action can blacken the sky when it is agitated by a comet.

The secret is that all these events are cyclical and the Controllers know it. They use this knowledge to re-set humanity, to cleanse the system and, to purge humanity off the face of the earth.

It goes without saying that when you have the knowledge available, you can control the weather. As a result, floods and plasma events become common causes for destroying life.

This book aims to introduce you to many of the clues that I, with the help of many others, have unearthed. It attempts to give answers to long-held questions that have plagued humanity for centuries.

These answers have come together from a bunch of people who have unselfishly shared their knowledge. Their sole aim in achieving this is to help humanity understand what being a human is all about and what we are, or were, capable of. As well as this, this book has been put together to give a possible answer to that biggest question of all - and the reason why I started this work in the first place:

*Do we live on a globe we've all been
conditioned to believe is real or, do we live
on a flat earth?*

Because we have found out what this place is about and the terrifying truth of it all, my guess is the game is up and they are about to reset again. Sadly, we, humanity, will find ourselves in the eye of a cataclysm.

What's going on regarding the great awakening is supernatural by nature and the reason why all this stuff comes to me is that the Creator wants me to find it. So, it is a gift to all of us and this is just totally mind-blowing to know. That said, I do hope you enjoy what is about to be revealed to you and that you enjoy this eye-opening experience.

1 THE RESET SYSTEM

Contrary to what we have all been taught, generation upon generation, this society living on this earth is a reset system. Oh, and it's been set-up by the Controllers.

It might be baffling if you are only just being introduced to this, but I'll bring you into the fold and reveal the information in a step-by-step fashion, so you can get the gist of it without going in too deep with all the details.

What is interesting for you to keep a note of, is that each 'survivor time' tries to reverse engineer the reset that the last civilisation went through. This could be why we have so many questions about our ancient history, questions that we have difficulty finding the answers to.

First, let me tell you, I am in a qualified position to know what I'm talking about. Cadw Welsh Heritage used to employ me as a Stone Mason's Assistant. I've also worked on a lot of archaeology sites, much of which was working on Roman buildings and amphitheatres. These have included the Roman baths at Caerleon and in Caerwent in South Wales. I have also been blessed to be able to visit Rome itself. When I first saw the Coliseum, all I can remember thinking was, "That's not 2000 years old!"

That was the moment the scales fell from my eyes and all the other pieces of the jigsaw puzzle began to fall into place.

Excuse me for using these kinds of metaphors, but they sum up what I'm trying to say, very well.

At that moment, as I stood before the Coliseum, I began to understand what all these symbols meant, and I started to find out where they came from. They were all clues. Clues our ancestors left for us. All these clues were linked to a civilisation that existed in ancient history, a time that we have not been taught about in school. In fact, we have been so massively discouraged to even believe that those people (with the advanced technology they had), existed at all.

So cunningly covered over were these clues that it was difficult to see through the haze. But, fortunately, the controllers were not cunning enough.

For a long time, possibly hundreds of years, the globe idea has been forced into our brains. It's been such a long time that it is now part of our unconscious mind. For that reason, it's hard to see through the lies.

Today, we don't question the reality we see around us. When we do, we are ridiculed for thinking outside the box on a subject like this and so we feel embarrassed to talk about it, which is only natural.

What we must never forget are the people who were tortured for telling the truth. You will remember from those lessons at school that people suffered in a lot of horrible ways, you've only to visit the London Dungeons to figure that one out. Can you imagine being hung or burned at the stake for telling something you knew to be true? Why would they do this?

The history books tell us that those who were burned at the

stake suffered that fate because they wouldn't agree with the church dogma at the time. They thought differently. They were independent thinkers. The real reason, I think, is that they fought against the new-fangled plans to hide what was real from people. They knew the truth, they disagreed with the stories that were being told, the lies about our past, the history that was being brushed over, and they were persecuted for it.

The thing is the clues they left all lead to somewhere mind-blowing. While this book cannot hope to have all the answers, it will help you begin to open your eyes and will ask you to question what is real. It will show you what the Holy Grail of our flat earth is. The Holy Grail of the biggest secret that has been kept from us for a long time is all to do with Technasma.

Technasma
Everything I present to you in my work is to do with Technasma. There are so many practical applications for it, both good and bad. This technology can save and heal humanity, it can make trees, pineapples and all kinds of food that we eat today, bigger than people. It can also turn on us.

You are given a clue as to the type of Technasma that was used, as it's there, in plain sight, in the statue that's on the front cover of this book. What follows is the brief story behind the photograph.

I was with a friend on my way from London to Norfolk when I saw the answer to everything I had been questioning for years. It was a statue of immense importance and in that one statue were all the clues to the history that had been hidden from us. It just stood there, almost hidden by the trees, and it was just waiting for someone to understand the secret meaning behind it.

I told my friend to stop the car. I jumped out and took the photograph. I had the answer and it was nestled inside the Empty Knight's armour.

Roman Fasces

The fasces are often associated with the Romans but, while they are not actually Roman, they are *the most important device in history*.

I believe that fasces are one of the greatest symbols in humanity and are on par with the Swastika. Mussolini used them as an emblem and they still are a well-known symbol for Fascism. How they originated as an emblem for the Centralised Control of Caesars, you're about to discover in this book.

Basically, fasces come in all shapes and sizes – small enough for Roman soldiers to carry and big enough for giants to hold. Yes, you read right, giants. The fasces depicted in many of the images our Hive Mind has found are huge. Too big for an ordinary human to carry.

They are not a quiver for an arrow or an axe and, for a long time, I wondered whether they were Gatling guns or even canons. But what you can be sure of is that they are always found on masonic pillars and big historic buildings. Go and look for yourself. See those grooves in the big pillars, they pay homage to the fasces device. Once you begin to see this, you will see it everywhere.

What Are Fasces?

When you look at them in old paintings, or marble friezes depicting battlegrounds and even in the photograph I took of the Empty Knight, fasces seem like a lot of sticks bundled together. They look like big rods, almost like tubes, made of copper or brass and they are bound together with what looks like metal or leather. In some depictions, it looks like snakes are wrapped around them. They can project horizontally, though they are not bazookas and they're not spears either.

The coil and cable

Today, we are told to unravel our extension cables. The reason for this is because of the electromagnetic field that builds up when you bundle them together.

The cables you see today, under the sea or even under your house, are made of copper, aluminium or stainless steel and they are tightly bound together with wire. Take a cable, any cable, and hold it up. Look at the end of it. You'll see that its shape resembles that of a round church window.

Churches as Technasmia devices

Church windows are based on more than cymatic patterns. Step inside any church and walk around it. Note what is

Rosslyn Chapel Window by BlueBudgie at Pixabay

under the round window. There's usually a huge organ. What do church organs have above them? They have what looks like hundreds of pipes bundled together.

These church machines have holes or, what looks like, portals in the dome to let out the augmented music. The music was used for our benefit through acoustic healing and other applications.

Water and Dust

Get your local map out and make a note of where your town or village church is located. Nearly all of them have been built near water. This is interesting because, going through the ages, the fasces relate to water and something that we'll briefly explore later in this book; Star Forts.

Fasces are not just found in images that depict Rome and Romans, but they are also described in the Bible, with Noah and Abraham. You can see for yourself that it's the same type of architecture as the Etruscans had before the Romans even entered the history books.

What surprises me is that in those depictions, it looks like nothing has changed; fashions are very similar, weapons are still arrows, swords and knives, buildings are the same Greco-Romano style. In the timeframe of what is supposed to span over 1,500 years, it seems as though time hasn't moved on at all. And you can't blame the artist of the time, as they are normally the talented and creative types who have documented history as it was before it vanished forever.

When the Romans marched to the front lines with fasces on their shoulders and took them into battle they were used to great effect. These were the original weapons of mass destruction. When you look carefully into the backgrounds of these pictures you'll see the battlefields and, more importantly, you'll see that they are burned to dust.

You'll always find that fasces are associated with the baton of army Field Marshals. Of course, you'll learn that this narrative is a false one. If you think about it, logically, you wouldn't take an entire Regiment into battle with sticks bound together, without it being a weapon of some kind to help them win that battle.

> *The idea behind the bundled fasces is that one stick can be snapped but, together, they can't be broken.*

An analogy for what the fasces represents can be found if you search no further than your own wallet. In America, on the US dollar you'll see the eagle and, in its claws, is a bunch of arrows splayed out. That's showing you what the fasces represent: power.

One good thing about the fasces is that there are many depictions of this device attributed to bringing health and well-being. Unfortunately, though, you'll be surprised to learn, it ties everything in with the modern-day weather, freak fires, hurricanes, snowstorms and heatwaves.

The Emblem for Fascism
Forget, for a moment, the actual fasces device and think instead about the shape of it. Think of the kind of logo that could be created from that shape and what, in your mind, that might have represented over the years. When I look at

the shape of it, I see the logo that the Fascists use on their flags. The fasces is an energy weapon so, when the Fascists fly this flag in their precessions, what do you think the message is?

We'll investigate them later and we'll also see other potentials for the tech.

Fasces and the Empty Knight
Fasces are nearly always depicted in images alongside, or even inside, The Empty Knight. The Empty Knight is a Roman Soldier's Uniform, mainly the breast and backplate of the armour topped by his helmet, often seen in paintings and images from the medieval period. The odd thing is, it's usually empty, there's no man inside of it. Just as you see in my photograph on the front cover of this book.

The fasces device can be found inside important, prominent buildings, they're used as symbols on logos and depicted on coins too. The fasces device is shown in a frieze above a door in the American Oval Office, it's on Honest Abe's chair, on the Memorial Gettysburg Address, and even in the House of Congress. The Fascists use it and it's linked with the Eagle of Control, too.

As well as the image of the fasces device being present on buildings everywhere, you can see it on Coats of Arms, both modern and historic, in the Courts of Justice and even when you see the orb and sceptre together as these play their part of it too.

The fasces must be significant because it's even depicted beside the US flag in the Capitol building which can only mean that it's more than just a symbol. It is as though the people who created the Empty Knight with the fasces device inside, have been trying to tell us something,

something that has a more profound meaning than we will ever know.

As for the Knight himself, where could he have disappeared to?

Of course, you'll also see that The Empty Knight carries inside him, an implement that looks like a lot of rods bound together. As with the fasces device that we've briefly explored, and those depicted in images of Romans before or after a battle, this implement usually has an axe head coming out of the top of it. The question must be asked why? Why would an entire regiment take this device into battle unless it was a weapon of some sort? The Empty Knight may be representing the uselessness of enemy soldiers, or how soldiers were turned to dust when the band frequency weapon was used upon them.

The depiction of the fasces is also shown in Napoleon's standard. And we all know how successful his armies were on the battlefield.

World Wars
In the First World War, Germany threw bombs at Paris. Naturally, the French retaliated and defended their capital from aerial attacks. In the photographs we've seen, they seem to have used electrical rockets to shoot down the Zeppelins. You would think that they would be firing from canons up into the skies. But no.

Fasces were not a canon made of a bunch of sticks bound together, but Fazer's. And the Fasces weren't bombs or bullets, but sound waves or what could be described as electrical beams. It may be impossible to believe given the period in history we're talking about but, it could even be described as a light beam or even a concentrated infra-red beam.

If these fasces were used on the frontline, what could they do if they were fired at people? Reports have said they had a harmonic resonance, a kind of sound wave. Because of this, and their inability to directionally point these weapons at a target, it affected their own people too.

But the most intriguing thing about these fasces leads us onto one of the main topics of this book and where most of my research hinges. It is on the one common theme of WW1: the mud.

Muddy Fields of War

More than anything else, apart from the immense and tragic death toll, what defined WWI was the mud. It was everywhere. Everything and everyone had to deal with it; soldiers struggled to wade through it, the bombs and shells just landed in it and fizzled out, the horses and their wagons got sucked into it and sank.

It was one of those uncomfortable facts of WW1, and it slowed everything down. With so much mud, it meant they couldn't move stores; food, bedding, clothing, etc. Anything that made life a little more bearable couldn't be delivered. This included ammunition too.

You will most probably have heard the term 'trench foot'. It was the most common complaint among the soldiers. They stood for hour upon hour in those miserable mud-filled trenches, so they were bound to suffer. They had to invent stuff to get the mud out from the trenches as there didn't seem to be an end to it.

*The official records say that it was
persistently raining and that is the
narrative we are fed today.*

So, the Germans were blasting sound waves over the
trenches in WW1 and the French were using electrical
Fazers. Who would believe such a thing as fasces existed
at that time in our shared history? I've discovered hundreds
of old books that discuss fasces and nearly all of them
describe these devices as an energy weapon.

The Horns of WW1

A weapon like no other

As a weapon, the applications of fasces are truly mind-
blowing, and all this can be tied in with this Technasma I'm
going to tell you about. But first, have you seen this image
of the sound weapon used in WW1?

It looked like a massive cannon with huge old-fashioned speakers, almost like horns. This was a sound weapon. The idea behind it was to use it as an anti-personnel device – it produced high-frequency waves that could burst eardrums.

The men of Hitler's war machine studied many horrible ways to kill people. One of them was with low-frequency sound. Their first experiments were carried out on unfortunate prisoners, those they classed as 'undesirables' who were taken from the streets. The records say these people (their guinea pigs) felt dizziness, pain, they had diarrhoea and their internal organs melted.

What I find intriguing, is that the Romans (and the Etruscans before them) seem to have perfected their ability to do just what the Germans were unable to; directionalise this highly advanced technology.

I have learned that a similar sort of technology, in the form of a sound frequency, is being used in our modern age on our young people and that there are, apparently, different frequencies for different age groups. Many youngsters have reported hearing voices while they have been stood on street corners or high-pitched sounds in their heads. The media is not reporting widely on this yet, but it is there.

Band Weapons
Another well-known sound frequency device, used in antiquity, was the drum. Weird as it may seem, the vibration of a drum has been known to cause earthquakes. It is not just the volume produced that causes the reaction of the earth upon the sound; it is its ability to reach the same oscillating frequency and doing so at the right time. Think of opera singers who, when the right pitch is produced by their voice, can shatter glass. Tesla's machine

was also known to do this.

There is an active denial system built-up to deter attackers of this secret technology. This technology can send a non-lethal beam, one that can cause a burning sensation on the skin. The wave penetrates the skin to 1/64th of an inch which causes a person to feel like they are on fire.

The key to any weapon's success is in its ability to focus on a target, in this case, they needed to concentrate the beam. To achieve this, an antenna was used to focus the invisible energy.

Batons of the Field Marshals

The batons held by Field Marshals provide a link back to when Roman Emperors held the power. The batons are representations of the fasces which, themselves, were in the shape of a baton. However, there is an important difference between a Field Marshal's baton and a Roman Emperor's, and that is in the use of it.

A Field Marshal's baton is used in ceremonies and to show who holds the power. A Roman Emperor's, on the other hand, was a destructive device that could kill anyone in its path. It is almost as though they have a button on it that they can push to destroy everything in their path.

If you look at a Roman coin from the last millennium, you'll see the fasces is depicted. However, odd as it may seem to some who have studied the academic history we have been force-fed we now know it is not Roman. It's just attributed to that part of the world and that mysterious part of our history. If you leaf carefully through the old history books, you'll find that Rome has been found to be located in many places: Constantinople, Moscow, Paris and Rome itself.

Rome is not Rome - it's the name of the
civilisation just gone

Medieval drawings, carvings on ancient architecture and descriptions in history books, show how the Etruscan civilisation, which preceded the Roman Empire, had the same equipment and weapon systems as the Romans had. This all points towards the fact that the technology available to the Roman Empire had been invented way before they ever rose as a powerful nation.

In the pictures available to us today, and some of those used in this book, you can see that the Greeks and Carthage had the same too. In reality, though, it was the Phoenician civilisation posing as Romans. Throughout *The Holy Grail of Our Flat Earth*, you'll find this fact coming up time and again. It's not Rome, as in Italy's Rome. You will find Rome is the civilisation we've learned to recognise and when I refer to, say, Brutus and his Roman Legions going into Battle with the fasces over their shoulders, I'm mainly referring to the technology and advanced weaponry they had.

Thunderbolts of Zeus

When you see the fantastic weapons they had, the whole thing seemed like they were 'God' weapons. In depictions of Jericho, where the Bible tells you the walls fell, it was at the sound of the trumpets. In other words, the sound *vibration*.

In Jericho, they needed to hit a specific frequency before their trumpets brought down the walls. I'm not certain about this but, in some images, you may even recognise a chemtrail. It is as though there is some sort of dual-engineering and it is a technical device or an aerial. In some depictions, it shows that this weapon is something that only an angel can operate. In other images, you'll see a person falling to the ground, as though they have just died.

What is so amazing is that the technology the Phoenicians used during the medieval period these images were created - looks like the same technology as the sound-directed weapons shown on a modern bas-relief in Russia. Again, those people, in those times, were creating sound waves. Amazing.

What you've probably noticed is that some religious street processions seem to be about the boxes they carry with them. Images of this kind of ceremony seem to be everywhere, even in the illustrated Christian Bible a painting that shows a box being carried around, called the Ark, with a device. It's there in the Middle Ages, it's there in Biblical times and it is carried by people blowing horns, making music and, ultimately, creating sound waves.

All over Mesopotamia, you'll notice the fasces and also objects with what looks like pinecones on top of them. This is all in the period of Babel as written in the Bible. When I first came across this, I was surprised to find the same tech everywhere. They are the same horns that produced sound waves that created all that mud in the First World War.

These devices are depicted on Roman coins, too. There's an image of Julius Caesar with the laurel leaf on his head. The Controllers appear to give this to whoever is in charge so that they can show they have the power of an active EM charge. For Rome, this was so important that they took it into battle with them.

There are a great many images of processions where people pay great reverence to strange deities. The boxes they carry in these images, seem to be empty. These processions appear to have the potential to encourage rainfall and, subsequently, mud. They seem to encourage the weather to change from sunshine to showers. From what I've found in the archives, I believe the weather anomalies play a part in this.

All the Atlases of 1733 I have in my library all seem to have a common theme and, when you see it, you'll know what I mean.

The trophies of the so-called Roman Empire can be seen to be technological devices. There are plenty of depictions showing Romans marching into battle carrying the fasces. The fasces don't have flames coming out of them as you would expect of a weapon of that period, yet, they have the ability to destroy buildings with what looks like just a bunch of tubes or pipes with an axe hanging out of it.

*It doesn't make any sense until you begin
to think of it as EM tech.*

Today, our scientists and museum curators collect electrical gadgetry from all around the world, all of it is antiquitech. We now know this, without a shadow of a doubt, because there are hundreds of 17th Century books proving Technasma is a real thing. We now know these weapons created an undulating mud, which rolled like the waves of the sea underneath us.

Cymatic Experiments

Stop what you're doing right now and log into Google or YouTube. Type in your search bar *cymatic experiments*. What you will see is a lot of videos showing you the effect a wavelength has on a plate. The experimenter has put either sand or metal, or iron-filings, on top of the plate. Whatever works well for the experiment is used. What happens then, is that a sound vibration, usually from a speaker, is put underneath it. When the sound vibrates, the landscape of sand or iron-filings on the plate bubbles up or moves to form shapes. It looks very much like a miniature world with hills and valleys, much like the ones you can see in the landscape around you.

With the amount of data available on this, you can be certain that the events that have happened in the past, through battles won and lost and the discovery of buildings half-buried, give you proof that mud floods were brought about through a waveform of some sort.

In other words, it could be the Serpent travelling through this place that resets it.

The Orb and the Sceptre

Imagine if you were able to hold that baton, or fasces, in your hand and see all the potential power available to you. You would give reverence to its power and you would look after it like it was some precious jewel. There are a couple of implements which are pretty much very similar to precious jewels and, most definitely, weapons of some sort:

the orb and the sceptre.

The orb and the sceptre are particularly found amongst the British Crown Jewels. These are treasured as symbols and they seem to have so much reverence. Why? Because they are devices, or weapons, that hold so much power. They can demonstrate the Controllers' power over the active charge.

Over time, the volume of information that has been collected points towards what happens in the moments before any oncoming catastrophic events, or times when an 'active charge' has been implemented.

In today's world of collecting data and statistics, you may see graphs that show you there is a marked change in people's personalities, their emotions and their mental health when the moon is in its fullest state. I've noticed that the overriding common theme is that people turn either in on themselves or against each other.

Aquatec - The Roman Coliseum

There is evidence that the Roman Coliseum, or Colosseum, also known as the Flavian Amphitheatre, was pumped with water. Tens of thousands of tons of the stuff. Some pictures show the Romans had mock battles in it - with full-sized naval ships.

To achieve this, they would have had to have pumped thousands, if not millions, of litres of water into these places. How did they do that without electric pumps? These are something completely different and I'll explain later what I think they are.

There is still much we don't know but recent ground-breaking discoveries have helped us to decode this stuff and learn what they know. But once you know it, it's hard not to see it. Even the obelisks and columns with the intertwining wires around them mean something and relate to this antiquitech. It's exactly like a modern cable - it is all Technasma.

Who are the Controllers?

The Jesuits, the Vatican and the Secret Societies under the Phoney Over Lords - they all have their origins in Phoenician society. The masses, us, don't know what it all means, or we can't understand what they are saying. It's no wonder we haven't worked it all out - yet.

Other devices like the one on the Tiber, 1733, shows Castel Sant'Angelo with giant aerials and it runs along the river from some recent event. A Star Fort is depicted on an old coin and a Roman raised garden is in an atlas from 1733. We see many raised Gardens in antiquity, and nearly everyone is aware of the Hanging Gardens of Babylon.

It's the only place left to grow when the gloopy mud is below.

Mud flood events are a certainty. The buildings, many of which are still with us today, get dug out over and again because they had the tools available to do that. After a mud flood, there always seems to be geoengineering of more people. In the old photographs, you'll see at first, the population appears sparse, then it grows quite rapidly over what seems a short timeframe of, say, a couple of hundred years.

For any of these human disaster catastrophes to be of any value to the Controllers, it has to be about the EM tech and the subsequent resets that are brought about by them. Believe me, this technology exists and it's out there.

You'll see all this evidenced in alchemical type depictions. What you find in these late Middle Ages depictions, up to the Eighteenth century, are strange beasts and demonic deities seemingly worshipped and sacrificed. There are some very strange customs all over the world. The reality we see today was not the reality back then.

So, the question is, what keeps happening over and over and again and, more importantly, why?

The Electrical Connection
It all seems to be about comets or comet controllers and the question has to be asked, are these Phoenician Controllers from another place? It is possible that they could be 'outside of time' without ageing, devoid of death. If so, they would wait in Melancholy knowing the outcome. Do they give us advanced tech and knowledge?

The original leader of the Mormons claimed to have been given a disc from an angel, which looks bizarrely like a modern CD. The odd thing is, it seems every civilization has some sort of angel visitation at some stage.

But these stories do point to some sort of clue with electric, which may be something to do with the angelic realm. What is electricity exactly and can we define it? You don't turn it into photons of light, I mean, what is electric, exactly? In the ancient worlds, or the language of that time, how would they have described it?

Today, we know electricity is energy. It is bright, it's white, and it's pure, and this is probably why people in antiquity thought 'electricity' was God.

Plasma discharge events are real. You can witness strange phenomena with thunderbolts, it's not what you think it is at all. The thunderbolt has a will of its own. Once a thunderbolt travelled through my grandmother's house, seemingly moving out of the way to avoid hitting her. It went through the back door, rolled down the street and exploded in the canal. It seemed to be conscious.

What is frightening is that this same electrical power could be harnessed against us.

Comets could be plasma 'creatures' which cause plasma discharge events, anything it would touch it would kill. Just imagine that power on the battlefield, or in a City, and the devastation it would produce.

Flat earth past vs Globe future?

What appears to be a big part of all of this is the brainwashing of everyone. Throughout much of our history, people were convinced they were on a flat earth. Then, at some point, the elite of the time covered-up that fact and changed the storyline by telling everyone they were on a spinning ball. Those who denied and fought against the new version of the world, those who tried to keep the reality of life alive, were tortured or burned at the stake.

*This message has been initiated in the past
few hundred years by the Jesuits under the
guidance of the Phoenicians.*

These people, the Phoenicians, have encoded goodness knows what into our reality. To me, they give the impression of being rotten to the core – just pure evil.

While this is true, all is offered to us, whether you take it or not. It is up to you. I think the society we have now is the result of everyone treating this place like trash, not respecting one another, not loving one another, not caring for one another. It's not their fault, because they've been brainwashed. They've been programmed and socially engineered to live this selfish way.

So that the information in this book can be used in a good way, we must become aware of the possibility that we are living in the Devil's playground. It doesn't take a genius to work that out.

*Thankfully the Flat Earthers are here and
we are just not like that!*

In the field of discovering hidden sciences, you get to know what this stuff does. But none is more revealing than when the secret science of architecture was discovered. It's known as Technasma and this changed everything.

2 TECHNASMIA

Buckle in people, you're going to need to. Your brains will be dust by the end of this. So we're going to start here with Technasma or, what we commonly call it:

Phoenicia.

If you want to understand why history has been kept from the masses, then you need to know about Technasma. Technasma is the technology of administering sound waves into the environment for the benefit of all. Or not, as has been established.

A huge catalogue of Phoenician science exists, and nearly all of them show this technology is real. There's no escaping it. It's out there and it's a whole new field of exploration that needs to be investigated. The possibilities of this type of Technasma will blow your mind.

Church Machines

When you study all the images, the books and whatever other clues have been left for us, the narrative is normally as follows…

Survivors from the catastrophe enter a church building and find all these pipes. These people seem unfamiliar with what the church organs are, so they carve slits in the pipes and turn them into flutes.

Of course, we don't know where these people came from, nor how they've managed to survive. If you're super observant, you'll note that the people in the photographs seem bemused and maybe even a bit lost.

Remember the fasces are as old as Rome itself. But from my research, Rome is not as old as we are led to believe.

Church Organ in le Havre by PhotosForYou at Pixabay

The keyboard, which was invented for the harpsichord or an organ, was a relatively recent advancement. Ancient Rome didn't seem to have anything like this and if they did, they didn't leave any evidence for it in the artwork they left behind. You can see the harp everywhere in Roman depictions, and there are other stringed instruments too, but there's no sight of any keyboard.

Organs are in churches. Churches are machines
So, what you find is you get pipes going horizontally out. You find this a lot, not going up, but going outwards. The official reason is the battlefield trumpet. On the battlefield, the trumpet is blown for a sound for a pause in battle. Hold that thought. A pause in battle.

Now, remember all that I've been talking about relates to water, that applies to this technology as well. It seems that most churches and cathedrals have got watercourses running through them. All-Star Forts are connected to water as well and this is confirmed by the fact that they are all located on, or near to rivers.

The Crown Jewels
The Crown Jewels are very interesting. They could tell you some history. The biggest diamond on earth, the African Star, sits at the top of the Sceptre, which is a large wand type instrument, a rod, with a curling wire around it, serpent may be, and a diamond, something that could focus a beam. But obviously, to be able to conduct an electrical charge, they would have to be made of maybe gold? Oh, they are! Isn't that handy?

They can conduct an electrical charge. And what you find is that these things turn up all over antiquity. And they're always on the battlefield. The British Queen Elizabeth has them.

Now, one of these jewels, I believe it might be on the Crown today, was worn around the neck of Henry V at the Battle of Agincourt on Friday, 25 October 1415. Henry's knights and soldiers routed the French. A terrible downpour had come and everything had turned to mud so the French got bogged down.

It was a mud flood.

So, what does this tell us? First, we must ask, were they weapons? Like the fasces, are these all in plain sight? Have they been there all along? I'm not saying the British Queen's Crown and Sceptre are working mechanisms but, who knows? However, from the research I've turned up, they have something to do with it.

Through antiquity, you usually see the eagle of control and then you see a Roman soldier with a laurel leaf-type crown on his head. Then, there's normally another person with a sceptre and a crown sat on a throne or seat and they are above everyone else. While another person always seems to have an orb in their hand and then you notice something devastating: everything behind them is destroyed. All those on the battlefield have turned to dust. Is it the orb and the sceptre that's doing this?

You usually find that they've got a jewel, or a crystal, for directionalising the beam. There's normally a snake entwining down, and it's made of metal. In addition to this, think of the story of Moses, when he held his cane - there was a snake wrapped around it. Now, you have to ask, was that a miracle? Or was it technology that we haven't been taught about? These kinds of implements would certainly cause a magnetic field.

The God Killer

What is the sceptre meant to do? What is it for? This can be a bit disturbing. They say it's the God Killer. Was it the original God Killer? The sceptre of the ancients was an incredibly powerful tool and in nearly all the old books it says it was designed to kill the 'Faceless Ones'. The Faceless Ones? Who are they?

The implement 'sings' to its owner, but it stays quiet when another nation approaches. So, it gives off a sound, a harmonic, or a buzzing. Only a device that's intended to be used as a weapon can do this.

In all the depictions, in all the official stories of what a sceptre was supposed to be for in the past, it was an implement that turned everything into dust. The sceptre was able to do this with a focusing beam which was controlled by a black crystal, and a shooting beam did the deed.

What are the possibilities you would need to turn something into dust? Well, we have so many. Think back to America's 9/11. The evidence points towards something that turned the inside of the buildings to dust. You can see in some of the photographs that there are tables and computers that have been cut in half. Almost as though a beam hit it, right through the middle of the building. Whatever was used, it seems to have been able to carve neatly through wood, plastic, metal and iron.

Can you recall any other situations where this devastation was brought about? Hiroshima and Nagasaki, for sure. All these disasters share the same devastating effects and in nearly all the photographs it's obvious that the streets are clear of debris while the buildings fall in on their own footprint. It's as though they seem to evaporate and turn to dust.

In 1902, only a year after Queen Victoria died, those buildings in Hiroshima were massive and skyscrapers were everywhere. Don't you think that odd for the beginning of the 1900s? And even more odd is the fact that the bombs they dropped in WW2, completely missed the financial districts. The Great Expositions would have been built only three or four years later.

For any of this information to hit home to you, you have to see that the Controllers have their hands on far more advanced weaponry than they are prepared to admit. The whole system is set-up to hide the truth from you. For instance, ask yourself, if the devastation that happened in Hiroshima was caused by an atomic bomb, would the General Hospital in Hiroshima (in the same city) have been able to stay operational throughout the entire time?

There are some examples in photographs, where you are supposed to believe it's the site of a nuclear blast wave. However, when you enlarge these images you can see people standing there casually smoking cigars. If it were a nuclear blast wave, debris would be thrown across the roads and down the streets. It certainly wouldn't leave roads completely clear. If everything was blasted, piles of rubble and rubbish would be strewn haphazardly across in the roads. It wouldn't be a photograph of everything missing, gone, vanished. Not dust. Not clear roads. Yet, it does seem as though everything has fallen into its own footprint. Why does no one question this?

American City Fires

Real fires usually burn uncontrollably. Fire Departments all over the world have a difficult time getting to the heart of the fire and some of those heroes die in the attempt to put it out. However, the fires that we're experiencing in modern-day, especially in California, share the same turn out of events as the atomic blasts in Hiroshima.

There are lots of sources, of videos and photographic evidence, that many people have published online their own personal eye-witness accounts of the California fires. These images often go against the official narrative that the media spews out.

When you see a firestorm, it normally rages through, uncontrolled, everything in its path is burned. But the images of the California fire disaster, make it look as though somebody has had a hand in it. In amongst the buildings that appear to have fallen in on themselves, are conifer trees standing tall and green on the verges, yet the buildings beside them have turned to dust. You can see where houses have been destroyed, leaving just the outline of their footprint. Everything looks like stone. How can that be?

Consider the devastating effects of the San Francisco earthquake. That shares the same scenario as the Lisbon, Portugal, earthquakes in September 2018, and the tsunamis that followed. But, not this one. I must ask, how can an earthquake be so strong yet, they'll relocate all the survivors down onto the beach on the seafront, and put them in the tents? Wouldn't they be expecting a tsunami similar to the one soon after the Lisbon earthquake?

All the events I've looked into seem to have been the same as Hiroshima. They all seem to have the same things happen: the streets are clear, and the buildings are missing. I repeat, everything seems to have fallen in on its own footprint.

San Francisco is not alone in experiencing this. Survivor witnesses everywhere, all say the same thing. That there were booming noises, or what sounded like incredibly loud artillery, something similar to sonic booms. But, this kind of phenomena has been attributed to subterranean activity, like earth activity, or they say plates. However, they all share the same story. After the booms are heard the devastation happens, then the streets are clear, and you see that every type of architecture has just disappeared.

In photographs of the Chicago fire in 1871, the whole city is gone and everything is replaced by a Great Exposition. When buildings fall after a bomb has hit them, you usually see rubble. But not in those images. Streets are clear and everything seems to have vanished. In photographs of Richmond during the American Civil War, the buildings are missing, the rubble too. It's almost as though the Hiroshima bomb had been detonated. But those photographs depict Chicago, in 1871.

Explain to me how fire can do that to
masonry anyway.

In my city, a few years ago, masonry buildings burned down. The building was there, but the inside was gone. In the photographs of the American city fires, the buildings look as though they've been blasted with something. It looks incredibly like 9/11. They have just disappeared and what remains is just dust. Penny dropping? We go deeper.

All too often, we are quick to look at the dark side, the sinister truths. Of course, as with everything in this life, there is always an opposite so, please do keep in mind there is always another side to it all. The possible outcomes of this are mind-blowing – and it can save humanity.

Ceremonial Maces

I've touched briefly on the ceremonial maces which are found all over antiquity. They're a type of sceptre and they are large. When you watch official ceremonies with governments or Royalty, you see the Parliamentary Master of Arms carry them when they officially open Parliament. If you get the chance, check out the black rod.

If it does nothing, why do they use them in official

ceremonies? Why give them such an important thing to do? Was there a time when it was able to do something? That's what we're going to look into now.

Hegelian Dialect

If you've been interested in this type of subject for a while, you'll know that all religious precessions in history have shared one serious coincidence. I don't believe coincidences exist.

It's the Hegelian dialectic: Problem. Reaction. Solution.

The sequence of events for all these religions processions is as follows:

- They had a drought
- They had a procession
- Then it rained

Ok. How many cultures have had these happened? It turns out most had the same thing happen to them. Crops were failing, people were going to starve. So, they bring some sort of processional alter out, carry it through the streets, and it rains.

In Venezuela, they had a very hard drought, they decided to bring in the Virgin Mary for a procession. After the procession, it rained heavily. This kind of thing happens over and over again. I don't believe it's down to Divine Intervention.

The clergy that conducts these processions, bring out these ancient relics to parade through the streets and are taking a big gamble. If they take these through the streets and it doesn't rain, people are going to lose faith in their religion. So, as the clergy are not supposed to be gamblers, they know that when they bring this thing out, it will rain. And they know this, over and over again.

Is it a miracle? Or is it something to do
with what they are carrying?

That's the Hegelian dialect. They create a problem, which is the lack of rain. They propose a reaction, which is normally a religious procession. After which, they get the solution, which is an abundant crop after the rains.

I've seen these myself in Sicily, Italy. I've seen all the people in the streets, parading around after this processional alter. But, at the time, I didn't take much notice because I didn't know what it was. To me, it seemed like some sort of celebration or party was going on. I soon learned it was something else and there was something more sinister going on.

Religious relics?
As you see in the image here, there are metal rods, holding up a cloth roof, with something on top of it. A relic. Now, these clergies have got to carry these things through a town. They seem to be very ornate, heavy metal rods to carry a cloth. Wouldn't it be easier to carry something lighter through the towns? Like wooden sticks, bamboo? Or something like that?

Check the twirl of the wire that goes around the pillars. I have to ask, would that create a magnetic field? And, with the obelisk on top, the whole thing seems to be a device.

The twirling or turning thing that's going on there, if it was a wire around a central column, it would cause a magnetic field. They're like sceptres, holding up a cloth cover. So, all these heavy metal rods, held by a lot of men, to carry cloth makes no sense. Does it do something more?

Why does it have to be metal? Why does it have to be a device? There may not be something happening with them now, in today's modern age but, there was a time when there was.

Religious Processional Alter by an FEB fan

Processional Alters

I have a *Leide Atlas,* one that I've presented many times in my YouTube videos. It's one of the best I've ever seen and there's a depiction of a procession with a man that's just arrived on the scene after a battle. In the background, the battle is depicted, and everything has turned to dust. In the previous page, there were Tartars and Cossacks and their horses' knee-deep in mud.

The Roman Emperor had a processional alter piece with a canopy, carried over his head. All of that effort just to carry a piece of cloth in the open air. Whatever it was, it left the enemy in dust and terrible trouble. It's the same in nearly every depiction I come across. The Romans go into battle, all hell breaks loose, and cities turn to dust. Everything is missing, all of civilisation is gone.

The *Leide Atlas* says all the images it depicts are located in Rome. Interestingly, when you look closer, you find that there is a Rome cross-over where you'll see people of Rome mingling with people of the Middle Ages.

In most of these *Leide Atlases*, you'll see the orb, the sceptre and these processional honours depicted everywhere.

Balustrades and Pillars

When I was in Italy, I remembered those columns on that processional alter and they played on my mind. They were bundles of pillars, bunched together, much like the fasces, and organ pipes. All of them look like groups of rods. Could they be of any benefit to humanity? Is this why they look like devices?

Keep in mind that they have the ability to resonate and they are made of a specific crystalline structure. You can also say that they look remarkably like gadgets, they are numerous and they emanate something like a sound wave into the ether. So, what exactly are they doing? For example, in Cathedrals, you have masonry pipes packed together. They look like the balustrades on bridges. Many of them are concrete or steel and they are bound tightly together. Why? Is that to create a higher charge, maybe? Is it a science?

The Hourglass

Apart from studying these pillars and balustrades, there's also the hourglass to pay attention to. This is an object that is depicted in nearly all images in the Middle Ages. For years, I believed it all to be just a coincidence that the hourglass seems to be in all these depictures. But then I noticed that they also have what looks like sceptres on their sides. How do we keep failing to recognise all of these clues? Are they supposed to have a deeper purpose, I mean, is it supposed to depict the sands of time or dust?

The Jewish Menorah

In addition to all these devices I've just mentioned, there are other examples of Technasma that must be considered alongside them. For instance, you might be surprised to know that the Jewish Menorah is one of them.

These devices are talked about often. They've got the horns and the box which is heavy, and it is carried everywhere - like the Ark. You've probably seen Stephen Spielberg's *Indiana Jones* film where the Ark kills everyone with a sound wave, this is similar to it.

There is some sort of an antiquitech device connected to the Menorah. They appear to be some sort of device as, again, they carry these things on processions in the open air and everyone has great reverence for them. They've got some balls on the top of it and it has coils around it. What if you knew it was possible to create a magnetic field? Once you are aware, you see them appear all over antiquity.

I have taken you through the different types of Technasma devices that could have been used, whether this was something that was to harm or heal humanity. In practice, this can only be classed as a theory. So, how do you find out whether advanced technology was put to use in reality? This is where it gets really interesting.

The Cloud Buster

The best gauge we can use to show that ancient Technasma was used as a real device, can be found in Dr Wilhelm Reich's experiments in the 1940s. Dr Reich developed a science where Orgon Energy could be used. Remember the organ and its pipes? Dr Reich's science was amazing as, with this device, he could create a climate where it would rain on cue, in the desert, simply by pointing this device to the sky.

There is a big difference between something that was used in antiquity, depicted in books, where no one is alive today to tell us if this was real - and one that was physically used, and its effects documented by scientists within living memory. Dr Reich's experiment was the latter. His device looked like a lot of pipes that pointed up to the sky. What is interesting is that his device used the same technology as the processional alters – and he created rain with it.

They're using an Orgon Energy.

There is a place in the device where water enters into it. Apparently, the orgon device needed water to top it up as this was part of its mechanism. It appeared to need an electrolyte of some sort. This is where Star Forts come into the picture and the reason for how and why churches are located near or on a water source. These devices can be rebuilt, and people are rebuilding them.

Think of the possibilities of all those waste grounds. The

deserts of the world and the arid land that could be replenished. All of it could be made into green pastureland for people to make food. There is always a bright side.

Mini Haarp

Right the way through antiquity they seem to have depictions of Energy devices. The Roman Empire thought they were important enough to carve pictures of them into marble friezes, and the fasces too. As I said earlier, you'll see the symbol of the rods, or fasces, under the American dollar, which is depicting the splaying of the energy field. And, you'll also see these arrows splayed out on the Rothschild's Coat of Arms, too.

Once these images become dormant, their meaning becomes lost over time.

These are weather modification devices. They are rods, except they are rods like orgon pipes and we know it as the Orgon Cloud Buster. But it is being used as a mini Haarp device. They're linked to the water which creates a whirlpool and a vortex that runs on an orgonite. It's all connected to pipes which appear to manipulate the weather.

Unfortunately, though these can be used to heal people, the Controllers are using it against us. They, sadly, are calling the shots with hurricanes, earthquakes, tsunamis, and all these bad weather events. They are all down to this device.

The open ends of these hoses are to be placed in water, says Wilhelm Reich about his Cloud Buster. The Cloud Buster consists of an array of hollow tubes, just like the fasces, the orgon pipes. It is a Technasma device.

Metal tubes connected at the rear, to a series of flexible support metal hoses in which are equal and slightly smaller in diameter to the parallel tubes. Alternatively, the rear of the tubes are joined together, the single largest diameter pipe and flexible metal hose to open the end of the hose in water. Reich believed this to be a natural orgon absorber.

So that's where the water is coming in the Star Forts. All around them, underneath them and right through them. Orgon absorbers. Part of it is needed. The pipes can be aimed into the areas of the sky and draw energy to the ground like a lightning rod.

Dr Reich's story is an incredible one and you should check him out. Unfortunately, as with many men who are about to create something for the benefit of humanity, he died shortly before he was released from jail. He was conducting science for the Nazis before travelling to America to work for the government.

There's so much we can do with this. Thinking about what we can do with this knowledge now, everything can change right now.

Orgon Energy
Nikola Tesla's orgon energy device happens to be four rods sticking up, horizontally, very much like the processional alters they are making rain with. Aren't the puzzle pieces all falling into place?

When you realise the word organ is used everywhere, it becomes clear that it's all about the vibration. You listen to organ music in a church – you feel the vibration. You organise and plan your life – and get good vibrations because you're happy. For your organs to be healthy you eat organic food. And then there's the good old one at the end, the sweetest one I think, the orgasm - for a happy life. Interestingly, Dr Wilhelm Reich wrote a book, *The Function of the Orgasm.*

There's a lot of information you can get on Wilhelm Reich and there's a film about him that is amazing. It focused on a story about some people in a desert. They had crops that were failing because of a drought. Dr Reich went there, put his machine up and, low and behold, the place was green in no time at all.

It's beautiful. It's real.

So, there he is, Dr Wilhelm Reich, and his invention. He pushes it up the hill in Kate Bush's video 'Cloud Buster'. He points it at the sky and gets taken by the government. Soon after, it rains.

We know what's going on. We know this is a real device.

The whole thing was completely swept under the carpet by the government after Dr Reich was put in jail. There are lots of films about him, it's not like it's a secret. It was plain to see what he was doing. Orgon energy and the weather is the flip side of the coin for the accepted science, you see.

So, if you get a beam, an intensity beam, in a battlefield, and you put it on the side of a fault, or a bank, into a watercourse, it's going to create mud. That weapon caused mudflows. The mud floods - they come, and they go. It's this science of Dr Reich's and it's a fact.

Sand Stone
In a video I presented, I referred to an atlas from Star Trek that shows maps of the world from the 1300s. And it shows the same as the Mappa Mundi that the Sahara Desert is not a desert. It's got deciduous trees and a mountain range called Kaong, running right the way through it. And

it's covered in palaces which look very much like the European buildings.

The Sahara today is a desert, and nobody has a clue where all that sand has come from. It's ever-encroaching, as all deserts are, but no one knows the cause of it or why it's there. Some people have said it was a nuclear war. So, when we turn back to the sceptre device, you'll remember that it turns everything into dust. Guess what the Sahara Desert is made out of? Not sand, but dust.

They always say, "There's a dust storm coming!"

Now, remember, most things that are built in that region are made of sandstone which could be turned into dust. I believe that there was an ancient civilisation in the Sahara Desert and that it was turned to dust by these weapons.

The Sahara Desert doesn't have sand, it has dust.

Another one bites the dust! Thunderbolt of lightning, very, very frightening indeed!

Yes, I know. Programming from Queen. Who knew?

3 FASCES

Understanding a Technasma device can show us how it works. Focusing on one, the fasces, and seeing what they can do, can take us to another level of understanding, but finding others reveals to you the variety and lengths that people went to so they could create these powerful implements.

In this chapter, I aim to make it clear how many of these things we can discover and what they might be capable of. We're going to focus on whether the fasces device was just a symbol or, more importantly, did it have another purpose? If so, what was it capable of doing?

The fasces device that I saw in the Empty Knight and now see everywhere I go, looks like a bundle of rods with an axe embedded into it. Mick Heart postulated that you probably had to press the axe head in and out so that you could agitate the device to kick it off. He used gallium as an idea for one of the electrolytes. I've seen gallium and it is amazing stuff because it can melt in your hand, just like mercury, and when you put it in a glass it turns into dust.

Realising that the fasces, as Technasma devices, are probably hidden from humanity for a reason, in this chapter I want to explore some other devices that may have been ramped up like the faces.

Antiquitech Towers

Many of the towers that you see in antiquity could have been used as antiquitech devices. What about the Leaning Tower of Pizza? It has an inner core and a spiral around the outside, maybe to create a magnetic field.

What about the Tower of Babel? There is no reason for it to have a spiral around the outside like the fasces device yet this building is attributed to a 'reset'. The people seemed to have been trying to get up to the top of the dome that covers this earth while asking, "Can we get out of this place before it becomes a blitz?"

Turris Babel by Athanasius Kircher

If this Fasces is a device and one that brings about the reset, why do people blame God for wrecking this place? There are images in the *Leide Atlas* that say it is supposed to be in Biblical times, in the Old Testament, Genesis. It's really in the Bronze Age.

When you look closer at the images available of the Tower of Babel, you see architecture that looks very Greco-Romano in style and, interestingly, in the image presented here, there's something that looks like cabling holding a flag. The place is inundated with mud and, the tower itself had a canon. If you know your history, you'll know that the canon wasn't invented until the Middle Ages. It appears they were building a machine.

The Tower of Babel looks like a machine.

Antiquitech Pyramids

There are also many antiquitech pyramids - the space age types of things with what looks very much like a dome on the top of it. These pyramids are supposed to have been built many, many thousands of years ago. In some pictures, you can see pyramids in what looks like a smashed-up place. Are these what we now believe to be the re-sets?

What are the artists conceiving and how long have they known about this? Some of the images and architecture from antiquitech would be considered futuristic now, in today's modern age. There's no doubt in my mind that some of these are machines reaching up to the dome. But then, if that was the case, wouldn't they have all killed themselves?

This is a big topic in my work here, the tower. In particular, the Tower of Babel. It could be thought of as an analogy for our time. Today, everyone in this realm is speaking a different language. The tower reaches up, and it gets bigger...

Now there are other buildings you could think of that have fasces attributions. One of them is the pyramid. Houdini put forward the theory that there was an internal ramp of some sort. After the French conducted thermal imagery on the Great Pyramid of Giza, what do you think they spotted? That's right, some spiral rows.

Now it's not an accident that some people use orgon devices in a pyramidal shape with a copper coil around them, inside of them and with gold on top. They are all part of the orgon energy which has many names. They call it a 'stupa' in China, and it has intersecting stars, very similar to Star Forts. One on top of the other, on top of the other, and they're all doing the same thing.

The Swastika
The Swastika was originally the Chinese symbol for orgon energy, which they call Chi - except they used it the other way around as the image was reversed for the Swastika.

It's strange how the Chinese have linked the sound of 'Oms' with that symbol and it was made for peace. Yet, the symbol was taken over, and reversed, for what seems like devious aims. The Chinese symbol for Chi energy represents two sides of the coin. People can harness chi energy and push them away without even touching them. I've done it myself.

There's the spiralling coil that represents the energy or, as in this case, the magnetic fields. The snake very often represents the coil. You'll see it in the emblem for the US, the column and the spiral.

Swastika embedded in ancient architecture by a Flat Earth fan

Remember when we explored the God Killer, the sceptre, in Chapter 2? It's not a God Killer as it hasn't the ability to kill God! But it does have something to do with rulers who had God-like powers and they were using this technology.

It's attributed to God-like power because it's electric, and it's linked to thunder and plasma charges. Think about it, if you lived in the 1700s, what would you have thought of someone had electric power, energy at their disposal?

Orgon Trees

What about trees? Do you think that maybe, they might be God's own Orgon Energy devices? They look very much like a pillar. In one of my vlogs, I asked the question, where these devices originally carved out of wood, like the pillar? Where they based on the tree? The trees, in this respect, could be seen as columns or flutes or straws, going down into the water. Under the ground, they sort of spiral, the reach up to the sky, reach out and collect something.

Are trees God's orgon devices? And is this where they got the idea for the technology from? Is this why they chopped all the trees down? A tree's roots reach down into the water and their branches stretch up to the sky. This is

Desert Cactus by Skeeze from Pixabay

probably where they got the technology from, and this could be what trees are. It's why you feel so good when you take a walk in the forest, or when you sit with one that's just outside the window. They're beautiful.

In America, there are huge trees. They're all over Europe, too. Britain used to be a heavily forested land but now we just have Sherwood, The Forest of Dean, The New Forest and a few smaller forests. Surrey is the most heavily wooded county in England but, as you know, now most of the trees in England were chopped down to build the Armada in the 1600s. All the trees were cleared, all the natural orgon devices.

So, God, in His infinite wisdom, the Creator thought, "We're destroying arid land so I'm going to need some of my orgon devices to bring moisture."

Our Creator thought up the cactus

The cactus is an orgon collected. It reaches up to the ether and resembles a lot of things in antiquity. But especially one. They're quite beautiful.

The Jewish Menorah
Its shape looks very much like a cactus/tree. From this, you can see that it's a device and that they've taken the design from nature - the trees.

I've got proof here now that they're using harmonic resonance, this Technasma, to grow fruit, food to be massive. Think of what that could do to feed the world!

The Menorah is a gadget. It's why they take it out into the open air in processions, this Chi, Orgon Energy is locked to the ether. If you analyse it a bit closer, you can see that it even shows you it's a device.

I think a lot of these things are attributed to the technology in the Old Testament. For instance, in Jewish traditional dress, there's a plate on the man's chest, and a block on his head. On that, there's some wording on it that talks about Armageddon.

Jewish Menorah by m3u1Kddw from Pixabay

4 THE WEAPON OF CHOICE

The Weapon of Choice

Much of what I've revealed to you so far isn't new and has been around for hundreds, perhaps thousands, of years. But, in our time, we've not been taught about the technology that our ancestors have had. Visionaries, such as Tesla and many other inventors of supposedly 'new' technological advances in the past hundred years or so, have known previous generations' technological advancements.

In this chapter, I'm going to be moving on from the dust mentioned earlier, the sandstone and dust in the Sahara. I postulated that the ancient symbol of the fasces was anything but a symbol and revealed it was a weapon that laid waste to civilisations. The remnants of the North African civilisation can still be found in that area.

What I'm going to explain now is how the fasces works, what it is and, when all of this is put together, what it can do.

To help you understand this, what I'd like you to do here, is to imagine you're in a park. It's a lovely little park. And it's in Sydney in Australia. Imagine you're sitting there, drinking, and you have a map on your lap and you see the lovely decoration around you and you're maybe listening to, or reading what I'm about to tell you.

First, we need some advice from an intelligent scientist, on how to get answers. In the German language, stein means stone.

> *"The scientists of today think deeply*
> *instead of clearly. One must be sane to*
> *think clearly, but one can think deeply and*
> *be quite insane." Nikola Tesla*

This is where you don't want to end up - tied-up in insane fallacy. We don't want to be thinking about black matter, unified relativity, reverse time, quasi neutrino flow, negative space, time-bending, quantum particles, or even picturing a microphone dropping to the ground as proof that gravity exists - and all other Einsteinian and NASA crap. That's just the start to give you an idea as to how we should think when approaching what we're going to be doing now.

In the text that follows, I am going to be thinking clearly, using facts and I am going to be doing it right. I'm going to be sane about things, not like some of these crazy-arsed scientists you could think of. It is quite a funny, but the serious point I'm making here.

A Plasma Discharge Weapon
In the previous chapter, I discussed the ancient fasces and after reviewing a lot of depictions of these, what became apparent was the huge amount that have the sword crossed behind or beside them. The images of the fasces that were presented in this era, always have the sword crossing.

I'm not entirely convinced the sword was used for cutting or stabbing people. More than likely, the sword was a plasma discharge weapon. With that, you would only have to touch your adversary with it to bring them down. There wouldn't be any blood squirting everywhere up the walls, and there would be no mess on the battlefields. It would just a tazer-like zzsth, and your adversary would drop.

While that might not seem likely, and most people have little or no idea as to how that can be possible, it can be put to the test. In our modern society, that's laden with lies we are beginning to see how everything that is taught to us is done in a backwards kind of fashion. However, the people who have unselfishly given up their time and knowledge to enable this book to be put together, have insights that can transform your thinking. They have given examples of scientific tests that can show if there's any reality in it along the way.

These people understood that the secret of the weapon of choice lay in the 'wings. Therefore, I'm going to take you through four things that point to this technology:

- The Masculine Sword
- The Feminine Labrys
- The Sun Symbol
- The Serpent's Wings

The Masculine Sword

Now the sword was a powerful weapon for the men in antiquity. I can safely say that we now know that swords were not used for cutting anything. A sword would be very difficult to use on the battlefield, you couldn't do much at all on the battlefield with them. So, 'on guard' - they are completely useless as a weapon of defence and a bit of 4x2 (wood) would deal with that very easily.

The cutlass of the sword of this era seems to represent a couple of things. I believe they can penetrate and, maybe, this is where the real reason for chainmail in the Knights of the Middle Ages has come from. What you need to do is have the steel tool next to the fasces and, by touching another metal object, you could discharge an electromagnetic current.

It may seem strange but stick with me on this.

The Feminine Labrys
This kind of technology is not new. We have found that fasces are related to electric currents and to understand how that is possible, we have to go back to the oldest form of electric currents, the Labrys. Below you will see an ancient mosaic from Anatolia in Turkey. So, the implement you see in her hand is called the Labrys. Apparently, it proceeds the fasces.

Anatolian Mosaic showing Labrys

The amazing thing about this is the woman in battle, with the usual thing with the breast showing. Do you think a woman is going to mount a horse in a pretty frock and go out into battle?

I'd like you to take note of the spirals in the shields. This image was found in Tuscany. Look at it closely, it seems they have very large people in those times. Were they giants using them in battle? Let's find out a bit more about these things.

What the Labrys has is four blades and always, there are only ever women in images with the four-bladed axe. But the odd thing is that there always seem to be doves sitting on top of the Labrys. Why would that be, if they were weapons of war? If it was a weapon does it make any sense? No. The Labrys device is surrounded by women.

American Dime Coin with Labrys

On this coin, you can see the Labrys again. It's just visible at the top on the left-hand side.

There is an underlying pattern to the Labrys device, and I've found out that it involves a lot of forecasting. When you understand that the blades represent the four phases of the moon the penny begins to drop.

The Labrys was a sophisticated moon calendar. Not only to predict the phases of the moon but the solstices and equinoxes of the summer and winter too.

How it worked was that you had to point it at the North Pole star, and then you could probably compare sizes and shapes of the patterns on the Labrys to the shape of the moon. All they had to do was point it up to the North Star and compare.

It's strange that this implement was held by women and that it relates to phases of the moon and seasonal patterns. But it's not strange when you know that fertility is closely related to the moon's phases. You had to be aware of how to use the calendar – particularly if you were going to plan for a family.

Interestingly, the lesbian movement has a flag and on it is a symbol of the Labrys. With their flag, there could be one of two scenarios going on here. Either:

- they've studied ancient Minoan mosaics
- the people who make the symbols know what's going on

Let's return to those fasces. I'm convinced when wrapped in a binding with metal rods, you can produce a weapon with them. Most of the images in antiquity combine the fasces and the Labrys so, and what do you get with this?

The Sun Symbol

If you look closer at the Labrys and the fasces, you'll see that there's a lion's head next to the blade. Sometimes there's a lion just above the blade and sometimes there's the head of an eagle just behind the fasces. Both are sun symbols.

Our research has dug up the fact that the moon and the sun are the same size, with a similar speed and trajectory. If that's so, then there's no surprise that the moon is depicted the Labrys with the lion and eagle sun symbols.

However, it becomes a different story when you see the eagle on top of a fasces device. When it's not nesting behind the blade of the moon, or above the blade, but on top of the fasces as in depictions on the US Dollar coin. There, the wings are splayed open.

I always wondered why so many religious institutions had the lectern with the eagle and its wings open. The eagle will always be depicted with its wings open. You are never going to see an eagle in its natural environment, flying in the sky or roosting in its nest. You don't see that. But you always see them with their wings splayed open, and not only that but a double-headed eagle as well.

You can see this depiction everywhere. Every time you see it from now on it will mean something different to you. There are thousands of pictures on my website, with eagles' wings spread open.

The Mystery of the Wings

The Egyptians were known to use another animal as a symbol; the serpent and, oddly enough, with wings. Also, they depict a lion-type creature that has wings and also a man with wings.

Iron Filings Experiment

So, what's going on there?

I started to ask myself what could be going on with these wings. Then, after an unrelated discovery, the moment of revelation came to me - which I'm going to reveal to you now.

This is an experiment using ion filings and two magnets in a jar. I only see wings here. What has just happened we've just unlocked the mystery of the wings, the mystery of the era. Would you like more of an explanation?

Iron Filings Experiment

What happens when you randomly throw iron filings onto paper with a magnet underneath it? We'll compare it to some emblems of double-headed eagles and see what happens.

The Magnetic Field

So when you see the wings outstretched, this is a reference to magnetic fields. When you notice this, it makes you look at everything differently.

It's even represented in the Egyptian Onc (Ankh). You'll see a massive pair of wings on that little bird, they're so big that it looks a bit strange. When you focus on those wings, a good approach to seeing the overall picture is to see them as the representation of a magnetic field. What do you think?

Think of these ancient depictions as we, today, use modern-day logos. The images represent something about the company. When it comes down to it, it's the idea of the magnetism that's the important bit here and what it's all about, is the power.

You could apply this to the depiction of the lady in power. It's the power, the lady is in power. Why? Because she understands how to control a magnetic field. You see the serpent as a wire wrapped around a central column of metal, it causes an electrical field. The eagle in the depiction, with its wings spread out wide, represents the magnetic field. The woman has the power. She has control over electromagnetism.

Now, it's interesting to see how the Christians depicted electromagnetism.

George and the dragon
When you see St. George and the Dragon, you usually find that he has a red cape on and he is spearing the dragon. In most images, when you look closely enough, you'll see it's not a dragon, but a snake with wings.

In this Russian depiction of St. George, it shows how he is controlling the magnetism. His red cape represents the idea of the magnetic field. You'll see that he's not killing a dragon, but he is killing a snake. Remember, the snake is a reference to the coil that winds around the column.

In other images, you'll see George and the Dragon with no red cape (wings) or even a magnetic field. Why is this? Because, the time when these depictions were created, the power had been transferred, or given over to the lizard. And the lizard has the wings.

The snake that coils around a fasces, or a column to create a magnetic charge, together with the wings that represent the magnetic field, would result in a fire. You'll begin to see how the wings on a cold-blooded reptile results in fire.

Now we know what the dragon means in these ancient depictions.

The Welsh Flag

Do you recognise the Welsh flag? It's the flag of my country, Wales. It has a dragon on it. But it's also the flat earth hidden in plain sight. You've got the sky which is represented by the white light of the sun. And you have the green part, which is the earth itself, divided by a flat horizon. Do you have any doubts?

Ayios Georgios (George and the Dragon) by Dimitris Vetsikas from Pixabay

Something extra - an Antediluvian Wall of Texas: a lost civilisation under Texas? So the town of Rockwell got its name from a mysterious wall hidden beneath the surface. So, in Texas, in the past, hundreds of years ago, there was a giant masonry below the ground in America.

We've just learned through the Labrys connected with the fasces, that this is a mini cosmos in your hand, observing the motions of the sun and the moon.

Welsh Flag by Dean Moriarty from Pixabay

We also looked at the snake, which is an analogy of the wire that goes around the column. Then the wings of the eagle which represents the magnetic fields. When you see the wings and the snake that's wrapped around the column, you get fire!

5 THE FLOWER OF LIFE

The last chapter opened your eyes to the outspread wings of an eagle and the snake as a representation of a coil around a central core. All of it shows you how this represents the creation of an electromagnetic field.

This is an idea that many haven't explored yet but, as I said at the beginning of this book, I'm going to take time and go step-by-step and walk you through these ideas.

In this chapter, I will first walk you through the meaning of the flower of life. Once you know the flower of life you will begin to see it in nearly every symbol of ancient and modern times and, more importantly, how it relates to the subtle energy of the universe.

You'll probably be aware of the idea of 'as above, so below'. Many globe believers think this applies to the aspects that govern the sun and moon around the earth. But I'm going to take you down a different rabbit hole.

To understand the deeper meaning behind the Flower of Life, first we need to explore the meaning behind the Russian Dolls. This is something that has been kept secret for far too long.

Russian Dolls

The common belief is that the Russian dolls are meant to

represent continuity as in, through a family network, like your grandparents, parents, children and so on. But this is not what they are.

Smart Russian parents give these dolls to their children. Why, when these dolls are not classed as toys? They are given to their children so they can get clued into the fundamentals of the reality we are living in, which is:

Perfect Nesting
The idea of 'as above, so below' makes perfect sense when you apply it to the idea of *perfect nesting*. As we go along this path, you'll find that perfect nesting also refers to the microcosm and the macrocosm. These Russian nesting dolls are a great way of helping you to think about smaller things fitting perfectly into smaller things. And vice versa, when bigger things fit into even bigger things.

Russian Dolls by Schwoaze from Pixabay

Let me take you a bit further along with this thought. We could even unlock the full secret here and now. Wouldn't that be good!

Cellular fission

We're not dealing with abstract mathematics, we're dealing with reality, and this cellular division is meant to be reality. So we'll go with that for now.

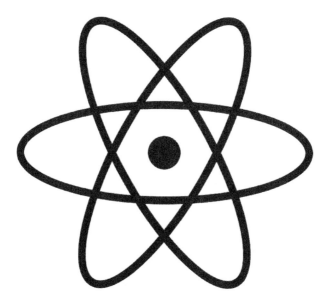

Atom by OpenClipart-Vectors from Pixabay

What you will find is that there are six phases.

1. the love between a man and a woman
2. the man and woman make love
3. male sperm fertilises a female egg and becomes a new life
4. then two cells become four

5. then four become eight
6. then on to sixteen

The most important thing to note is that crucial moment when one cell separates into two cells. This is the real, as above so below scenario. What is witnessed in one cell is perfectly echoed in the second cell. It's doubled again and again into the Flower of Life which refers to the simple rule of doubling every time.

I did say there were six phases, well a way to link this to the reality we're speaking of is to consider the six days of the week. Of course, we know there are seven but, this is an analogy of on the seventh day God rested.

The Flower of Life

When we speak about the Flower of Life, or the Eight Spheres as it's generally called, there only seems to be six and one in the centre which makes seven. How can it be eight? We'll get to that.

The Flower of Life is very important to our reality. When you look at the artwork of the ancient civilisations, they knew all about it. They always referred to the all-important eight sphere stability – the moment crucial for human existence. The eighth stage is said to be needed to grow to an adult human being.

Now, what follows is where it gets really cool.

The Star of David

The Flower of Life represents the cellular division at the crucial eighth stage. When you draw a line from the centre of each sphere, in a 2D world (the flat paper world), you'll get the Star of David - which is a hexagon. Once you see this, you'll begin to see the Star of David is an eight-sphere representation. In other words, a cube.

What I'm saying is the eight-sphere Flower of Life is represented as a cube.

Now I did say there were only six spheres, and one in the middle, so how are we getting eight?

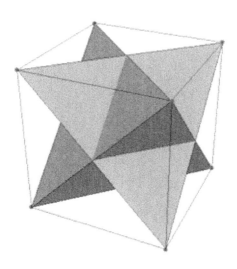

The Star of David as an 8-Sided Sphere

One cell is in front of the six.

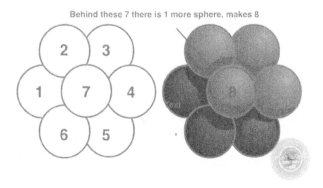

Behind these 7 there is 1 more sphere, makes 8

8 Cell Structure'

When you look at the flower of life in a 3D representation, it becomes clear how we can interpret it as a sphere.

In the next image, we've drawn a line from the peak of the top of each point and you can see the Star of David. But, to simplify it, clear your vision and it can be seen as a cube.

So, let's talk about the cube a bit. There seems to be a big emphasis on this in antiquity. A lot of denominations and faiths keep talking about this, that's for sure.

You'll see on Jewish people in their traditional clothes, have a cube strapped to their forehead while they read the Torah. The Freemasons, also, have an obsession with wooden ornaments too.

Image of The Star of David as a 'cube"

It's not only the Jews, the Freemasons and the Christians, that have a crucial role. But Muslims too.

The Muslims' Mecca

What you see at Mecca is a large black cube in the middle of an arena that's covered by a cloth. Do you notice anything familiar about this image?

In the four corners, there are vortices. Exactly like the Christian Bible version of our plane, with the four vortices in each corner.

It's a flat earth map. However, this is a Muslim depiction, so what's it doing here? I would like you to make a mental note of this, as you're going to need it for later on.

Kaaba, Mecca by Konevi from Pixabay

The Buddhist Buildings

We see images of churches (or should I say church machines?) in India that are often the shape of a semi-sphere with a dome on top. At each corner, just as we witnessed on the Kabbah, there are the four vortices, or four towers, surrounded by walls. What do you think this is? A cube. We have more to come!

The American Alamo

Have you seen the bank in Alamo, Texas, USA? It has something to do with the cube and we're going to get to the bottom of this.

Boxed Hour-Glass by Oberholster Venita from Pixabay

The Atomic World

What about in the world of atoms? I'll explain this as best as I can. If you take two squares and place one on top of the other, then turn one of them 90 degrees you will get a familiar shape, one that's used often in architecture. You see a lot of this shape that in Arab symbols.

That shape we've just described is in the 2D world, what you need to do is imagine it as a cube in the 3D realm. That's the world we're living in. What does it look like? What you get is this…

We know now where the Flower of Life's origins began - look what we've arrived at. Let's go a bit further.

Atomic fusion

The next stage is a chart of atoms going through a similar rule of division as explained above. You get the single atom, then the two, four and onwards. Here we go again, the same living cell formation with atoms, the perfect nesting. You'll see this echoed inwardly and outwardly.

Like the living cell that constantly divides itself, it seems there's a rule of initial opposing forces which are always kept. Then, from there on, depending on energy levels and the number of electrons, the shape can take many forms. But the most stable is the one in the shape of the cube.

Atomic division and fusion by Colin Behrens on Pixabay

The actual shape of our universe is an initial jewel shape – a cube.

What you get is a basic bi-polar shape. The basic characteristic is as two magnetic fields opposing each other.

Now I'm talking about atoms, not about down on the Planck level or anything in the sub-atomic realm. As that is insanity, and we're thinking clearly.

What you see in an electron cloud are two torus fields. Atoms are not a solar system; atoms are torus fields. This is a big knowledge to know.

Octet Rule

There's a basic rule that comes with official atomic science. It's called the Octet Rule.

If you imagine the central core to be a magnet, you will always get two poles. You will always get eight on the second. On the third, for some strange reason, you only get one electron.

In academia, there's always something of a joke among the students about with The Octet Rule:

"One does not simply... exceed the Octet Rule"

So, we're going to go with that.

According to scientists, nothing can exceed the number eight. The number eight is everything to the scientific world. Think of how many analogies there are about it, you've heard of 'infinity' haven't you? Once we understand the smallest of the microcosms of atoms then we begin to understand everything about the universe. It nests into smaller or bigger universes, and this idea of nesting goes under the number 5.

A Torus Shape – by Pete Linforth, The Digital Artist on Pixabay

The Golden Number

Five is the Golden Number and it is 100% pure evidence of our Creator. The Golden Number 5 is used to calculate vortexes and torus fields, but we'll keep it simple here.

Scientific principles say that everything in the universe must have this shape and the shape is a central core with two opposing clouds. Two magnetic fields, with eight more clouds - four above and four below.

To get a correct flat earth model, we have to consider this shape as a first possible shape for the universe.

As energy levels rise, we get a frame of eight magnetic points which look like an eight, or two B's standing back-to-back. Or, if you look at it another way, it's the number three. This is how it must work, and the elites know this 100%. Fix the image of back-to-back B's or 3's in your mind as this is important.

The number 3

Some of you in this field will recognise the sinister Disney Club 33. Originally, it was 83, then it was changed to 33. So when looking for its meaning, as in anything to do with 33, this would be recognised as gematria, where you can look at the 33 Masonic Code which has deeper connotations.

If you turn this symbol 90 degrees on its side, it doesn't look like 83 at all. It looks like a torus field. Too much of a coincidence? It could even be the North Star over the top of the two torus fields. As above, so below.

Incidentally, if you split the figure 8 in half, and you get two 3's facing each other. The true meaning of 33 is showing opposing magnetic fields or opposing torus fields. The elite put this knowledge in all their logos. There are plenty of them to see in the world. You don't have to look far either.

The broadcasting network (BBC) has opposing 3s. There's also a 70s band that uses the Bs back to back, ABBA. They never created this logo; the Tavistock Institute did that. ABBA has double Bs, back-to-back, these are opposing magnetic Bs.

When you know this, you'll see it everywhere. On an old Russian coin is the fasces with the bond. This can be interpreted as a ribbon or a rope, what matters is the fasces and the bond. Two opposing vortices.

In the Senate, these people rub it in our face so much, they have the two fasces and the laurels, opposing. They are opposite polarities or mirror images. When you realise this, it couldn't be more clear to see. It's all in plain sight.

But it goes deeper.

The laurel leaf

The Laurel is the snake – reference to the binding or bond (James Bond) that winds around the fasces and it's this that creates an electrical charge.

Do you recognise it? It's the Laurel leaf of the Caesars. We've worked out what this is, it's been apparent for a long time, when you consider all the sayings that you know of, like 'sitting on your laurels', or 'the laurels of control', where else would you these be used and where else would you see the link between the two magnetic fields?

The UN flag

The true meaning of the laurel leaf is in the opposing 3s, or 33. They represent two opposing toroidal fields. They also refer to the thirty-three sections on the flat earth map which is surrounded by a torus.

Also, the ribbon that ties the laurel leaf arms together refers to the bindings, the all-important bond that goes around '3' corn or wheat chaffs. When you look closer at what it represents, you can see the symbol of the hammer and sickle.

Last in this – where do you think the idea for the images on the American Dollar came from? They represent the magnetic fields or the laurel around the fasces.

~ + ~

I know this seems like quite a lot to process, but I'm sure you should be starting to visualise it in your mind. All this evidence is helping us to figure out the accurate, true and de-bunkable model for our flat plane. It has been encoded all the time through antiquity.

Thank you Technasma you've unlocked everything.

The UN flag by ChickenOnLine, Pixabay

6 MAGNETISM

All followers of my YouTube channels will know that lots of people are trying their best to stop this information from getting out. But persistence overwhelms them, especially when it's accompanied with real information and the truth.

One of the biggest questions that has come about on this subject has been about the fasces. What could it be? Jon Levi says what could it be. Maybe we could let you into the secret.

It seems that wings represent magnetic fields and that serpents, and Mount Meru in the North Pole, are all connected with magnetism.

A magnet has a North and a South polarity. I established that I believe this place is a double toroidal vortex with an inertia flat plane between the two. Like the atom, I explained in the previous chapter, the one with the nesting. When you consider all the evidence, it's the only way this place could exist.

Magnets
Magnets can be quite incredible things. When a magnet is not magnetised, it is stable, or still, that means the atoms are jumbled around and in a mess. They bounce into one another.

When you see a meteorite fragment, it's magnetised. To make them magnetised we need to align the atoms. They all have to point in the same direction.

- Atoms in a jumbled mess = inert, still or stable
- Atoms in the same direction = magnetised

This is quite important to make a note of, and all that follows is too.

Atoms in a jumbled mess – still or stable

It's important that the magnetic field is invisible when the magnetic flow is created. It's also important to know that all magnets exhibit bi-polar, north and south.

If it's snapped in half, will we get a monopole? One north and one south? No! I'm afraid not. That will never happen in our reality.

If you snap it into two, you're still going to get a north and south. You could go down onto the atomic scale and you'll only get the same north and south.

Poles in Pairs
North and South poles always appear in pairs. Attempts to

Atoms in an order – Magnetised

separate them result in more pairs of poles. If we continue to split the magnet, we would eventually get down to an ion atom with a North and South Pole. But they still cannot be separated. No matter how much you break them down they will always keep their north and south polarity.

You may have heard this saying:

Ordo Ab Chao

Or, 'Order out of Chaos' – it's talked about a lot because it happens to be a Masonic message. You need to begin to start thinking for yourself and not watching these people. They are lying and are here to misinform you and wrongly direct you.

Order Out of Chaos

They will tell you this is part of the dialectic of the New World Order. Not in this case. There's something else going on. Think of the wings of the eagle you see in statues of importance.

You see the 33 in the two torus fields in the following image. The highest Masonic place is in fact at the top of the pyramid. You will see the arrows pointing out and up in different directions, this means that this is not magnetised yet because it's going all-in different directions. You can see how they represent the open wings of an eagle.

This image lets you know that they have power over the electromagnetic field. They make order by putting the arrows in the same direction. This is the true meaning of Order out of Chaos.

It's a similar message to the depictions of St. George controlling the Dragon and the snake, they're showing you that they're controlling electromagnetism.

If we want to understand what the fasces were and very well still could be, we have to understand magnetism and magnetic fields.

Magnetic fields

Have you ever been in a science class at school and seen how ion filings react to a magnet? It's a standard magnetic field. But what you've witnessed was not the actual magnetic field. It's the position where the magnetic power finds and rests between the waves of the field. The actual waves themselves are perpendicular to these lines like this:

Now, in case you didn't know, this is important for where we are going. Turn this image ninety degrees, rotate it, and we get this:

What you're looking at are the two toroidal fields/vortexes. The North and South, just like the atom and the inertia flat plane equilibrium, that rests between the two.

We are all aware that a compass will point to the North Pole. So, there's something magnetic there. We think the North Pole is Mount Meru, but we can't get there to verify this. And there's a South Pole, the common consensus is that there's a South Pole basically beyond Australia and

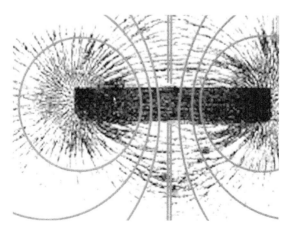

Magnetic Torus Field – Order Out of Chaos

beyond some sort of ice ring.

But that's not it at all. That is not what is happening.

There's no way that the magnetic charge is going to go from Mount Meru, 15,000 kilometres to travel outside of the circle – or outside of Australia - to where we are taught that the South Pole is. It's just not there. It's below ground level.

Mount Meru
Mount Meru, I believe, is a pyramid and it is above the earthly plane. The South Pole is below ground level, below Mount Meru.

When you look at ancient Babylonian depictions, they pretty much sum it up. What's happening is a stepped pyramid (Mount Meru), is the magnetic field. It's quite stunning. You can imagine two pyramids: one above ground level, the North Pole, and one below the inertia flat plane, which is the other half of the pyramid, the South Pole.

Gravity
It's not, 'small mass is attracted by a big mass'. This is not two bowls in a shed, this is not Cavendish. Gravity is a theory nothing more. What gravity represents is a magnetic acceleration acting on all objects:

- One from above, pushing down.
- One from below, pulling up.

If they are equal, gravity is cancelled out. That's what we get when we look at a mountain. It's still because it's on the inertia plane. Gravity is acceleration coming up from below and the one coming from above has cancelled it out. This is the only way this plane can work.

Here is a model to help you visualise. It's of two gravity wells or two density vortexes. There's no such thing. There's gravity. The model is actually an atom. It's the same, it's nesting and has worked its way out.

What you see is a model of any atom in
the universe.

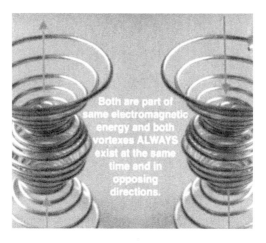

Gravity Wells or Density Vortexes

So, we have two torus fields with two opposing fields. They are two vortexes acting in opposite directions, simultaneously. This is a biggie in understanding any forces that could be referred to as gravity.

You have both a part of the same electromagnetic energy and both vortexes always existing at the same time and in opposing directions. Explanations in a book can only go so far, but you can watch a video animation on YouTube to see how this works. One arrow goes clockwise and pushes down. Imagine a screwdriver you're pushing it down and then it contracts at the bottom. With this example, I'm trying to show you that it passes through the North Pole hole and expands on the other side below.

Meanwhile, it goes in the other direction too, when it contracts. This is how a double vortex work. Does it remind you of anything? How about the Holy Grail?

So, did we just find it? Is this what it's all about?

You may have seen this on my vlogs, a lot of people talk about this. In essence, it is two opposing torus fields with a passage between.

Caduceus
Now, what about the Fleur de Lys? The other way to show a double torus field, or double vortex, at the convergence of Mount Meru, is by showing two snakes intertwined. You have probably seen this, but not taken much notice. Now you will.

The Caduceus is another word for Love and it's associated with health. Incidentally, the British health service uses it as an emblem. But what we've seen is that the Catholics and the Orthodox use images with a Caduceus between them. So, it appears they are complete opposites coming together, or converging.

You can also see it with two lions guarding it. It's an image that's used all over antiquity. It represents the convergence of Mount Meru.

A church in Texas uses the image of the double-headed snake. There's the curling of the staff in a screw, which reflects the vortex path of the magnetic wave. It ends at the top with the double-headed snake.

This is how the Creator made it possible for us to live in a constant balance. Here's a depiction of Mount Meru from an ancient Chinese depiction. It is two opposing torus fields, or atoms even. Basically, it represents two pyramids, opposing each other.

The Holy Grail in a lead window of a church

Ancient Chinese Bagua by Gordon Johnsonon Pixabay

The image that follows is a Buddhist depiction of Mount Meru. Again, it's the same thing, the double vortexes pointing in on one another. I think that the lower level of the pyramid is below ground level which gives us the South Pole and the North Pole above level. The beautiful thing about this is that it's showing the magnetic waves coming out in the shape of a sunflower or the lotus flower. It's stunning. It's the double vortex field showing in that image. But more than that, they've literally cut it into four sections as well – the four corners.

The Garden of Eden

In an ancient depiction of the Garden of Eden what we see is a round wall, which is like Mercator's Hyperborean, around four continents. Inside, there are rivers running up to a large magnetic mountain. And what's more, there's a

Ancient Buddhist depiction of Mount Meru

lake in the middle

Was Mercator crazy? It was just a painting, and he was just an artist, how could he possibly have known about all this.

So, what you see in Mercator's map of the Hyperborean, the continents and, in the middle, a mountain, is the magnetic mountain of Mount Meru.

There's a huge mountain in the middle of a lake which is

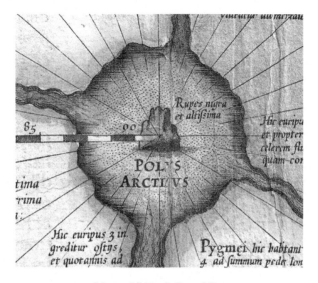

Mercator's Meru, by Rupes Nigra

lowland. How can you have a mountain in the middle of it? Well, this is going to rock your boat, I mean, Noah's Ark!

Think of magnetic waves travelling, like the ripples following a stone after being dropped in the water. There's a hole, a well and it peaks pyramidally and dips down below. From this, it's possible to have a lake and a mountain at the same time.

A hole, a cone and a pipe

You see what's happening, a hole, a cone shape and a pipe - all at the same time. Now, Mercator must have known this as a reality as this is the only way it could be. At the same time, in the centre of the flat earth, there's a lake in the middle, a huge magnetic mountain and a pole.

So, is there anything in the real world now that we can see, because naturally, I can't get to the North Pole to take a look, to see if this is happening. But is there anything that I could lay my hands on that would be just like Mount Meru? It turns out that there is.

Frequencies

Cannily enough, they can be found in car speakers. They are amazing things. The shape of the small tweeter in the centre gives you a very high-frequency tone. What are the chances?

Put a picture of one of these speakers next to the image of Mount Meru and you'll get the idea that Mount Meru gives off a very high frequency. If you want to make a God killer, you have to understand this. You have two options.

- Option 1: put magnets together, North, South, North, South. You're going to end up with a very long magnet.
- Option 2: put the magnets alongside each other and they will repel. Unless you bind it together with something. Like the fasces.

So, the fasces are magnets and the potential for them is incredible.

I recommend that you search out and watch a man on YouTube, called *SuperMagnetMan*. What he shows you is how you can stack pyramids in the same way you can with the fasces. He does it in the way that you can stack little pyramids and it creates thirty Tesla powers. That's around ten thousand gauss. That's a huge amount of magnetic power from perfectly nesting pyramids.

Nesting magnets with a bond to magnetise it with the fasces could create a huge amount of power.

One of the biggest questions on this Flat Earth British journey, is about the obelisks and pyramids in antiquity. Do they have the capacity to do the same? If they did, they would have to be made out of metal, not stone as crystalline structures don't just crack it. However, could they have been mechanisms, obelisks and pyramids.

Electrum

Electrum is a gold alloy, green gold. It was used in the old Kingdom of Egypt and it was this element that was used in the topping of the pyramids. What I've always questioned is, why don't they teach us about this in school? In college? Why do they keep this stuff quiet?

I believe these were the devices stolen by Napoleon's troops when they were there shooting the face off of the Sphinx, or whatever the story is. But I think pyramids could be electrical conductors and more. The Egyptians couldn't have uses 'hocus-pocus', they must have used Electrum.

The obelisk and the pyramid can be electromagnetic devices, and this is how it can happen. What follows may seem complicated, but all will eventually make sense.

There should be a way to nest magnetic fields in a way that their waves push in one direction. Directionalise magnetic waves. This sort of thing can only happen if waves can nest.

A site called ResearchGate.net, even shows you how they nest in a pyramid and an obelisk.

The pyramid and the obelisk

We can't check if, inside the obelisk and the pyramid, they were doing any nesting, but the proof could be there. If the nesting is carried out in a particular way, inside of the pyramid, this nesting process can be amplified. It's this that could be turned into a canon or indeed an antenna for waves. For an exponentially huge amount of power.

The question is, how do we store energy in a pyramid? To nest in a pyramid there is only one geometric shape that will nest in one. It's the Icosahedron, which is a twenty-sided shape, and it's depicted in an image called *The Melancholia*. Google it.

That can fit inside a double-sided pyramid. There's a geometric shape inside, which seems very complicated, but

Icosahedron by Klaus Scheiber on Pixabay

it's quite simple. It needs to fit perfectly inside a pyramid.

The only geometric shape that will fit inside a *double pyramid* is the Icosahedron. Remember the inertia plane comes between it - the top pyramid being Mount Meru and Meru being below ground level, the South Pole.

You may note that the shape makes room for a gap and that it won't fit snug or perfect. The reason being is, if you turn the Icosahedron ninety degrees horizontally, the highest corner will touch the next three corners. It's what you might recognise as *perfect nesting.*

Since you can nest up to four waveforms as you've seen in the depiction of eclectic waveforms, this means that you can send up to four different waves. Two up would spin up, and two down. That's monumental!

The elites have put these images outside, on show on public buildings. The Icosahedron is on the reset depiction.

In a pyramid or an obelisk, there can be four perfectly nesting waves. These can be resonating and due to the pyramidal form as it resonates, the energy will multiply. It is this energy that can be used directionally. On the spot near the pyramid or stored and used for later.

The key to it all
To store pyramids up inside to create these energy waves, the pyramids need to be stacked. This was a bit of a mindblower when I first realised this. The key is in the perfect nesting. It's collecting and storing energy which can be stored nearby. It is possible and it has been and is being done.

This is what makes square energy devices. There's your pyramid. If you want to create an energy device, the only way to go is not with the Egyptian pyramid, but with the Mayan pyramid. The step pyramid provides for nesting neatly inside of one another, for energy. Just like the Russian dolls. These reveal to you how energy waves can be nested, accelerated and transmitted and can also go in reverse and, can receive waves from the ether.

The cartographer Mercator depicted the North Pole as having an island split into four parts with the middle as Mount Meru. Could the energy of perfect nesting of magnetic fields in a pyramidal shape on Mount Meru be the reason for the four seasons?

There's a pyramid, I believe, on Mount Meru and there are two of them, one underground creating the South Pole, one above ground creating the North Pole. I believe them to be man-made or manufactured as they can only be artificial. This goes a long way to explaining any effects that are commonly known as gravity on our plane. You can put it all down to density and buoyancy.

This explanation also appears to clear up the inertia plane where we are now. The earth upon which we live has to be at an equilibrium between two torus fields. This is the only way our universe, or where we live, can exist.

~ + ~

Einstein with Charlie Chaplin (another Tavistock person) (CC = 33)

Albert Einstein said to Charlie Chaplin:

"You know what I admire most about you Charlie? It's your universality. The whole world understands you, though you don't even say a damned word in your movies."

Charlie Chaplin replied:

"True Albert, but your universality is bigger – the whole world admires you even though every scientist knows there's not one damn truth in any of your theories."

Busted!

~ + ~

This came up, concerning the fasces. The Faggot. The fasces is connected with the word faggot – a bundle of sticks or fags (slang for cigarettes in the UK) are lots of sticks bundled together.

7 AS ABOVE SO BELOW

I explained that the place that we live can only be between two torus fields. In this chapter, we're going to get to real answers. Some aspects to this are undeniable, and I just think to myself, how can any anti-flat earth globe channel (there are plenty of them out there) debunk any of this? I would love to know. Because, with the evidence we have, it's not going to be possible.

In my YouTube video (search the name above, or look in the Reference section), I show a map from a website where the temperatures and tides and magnetic declinations are revealed. They also kindly put an anti-ruffle equidistant flat earth map up for us. Very kind.

Rediscovering old ideas

When you look at that map, you'll see the magnetism over the North Pole comes out in four great loops. Just like Mercator's map of projection of the Hyperborean, or the North Pole, four continents split. You get the same with the magnetics.

But in the YouTube video, I show that their magnetics almost completely cover the Asian continents, all of Europe, Africa and America. Why is that? What could cause that? The magnetic anomalies that we witness over our plane.

If Tesla was alive, he could help us out. As I've said all along, I believe that Tesla rediscovered the information or the invention as he was a clear thinker. But the fasces technology we know is ancient. We know that all the technology, Technasma and antiquitech, have been there all along, so this means that Tesla rediscovered it all by clear thinking. So where could Tesla have got his ideas?

Tesla was Serbian. We looked online and we found a Serbian cross from antiquity. We need to look at this because it appears to have become priceless and I don't mean its monetary value, I mean the information it holds.

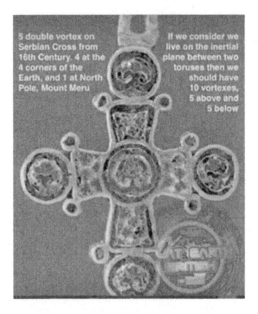

The Serbian Cross

Tesla had a standard education in a normal Serbian school so there was nothing particularly grand about his education. The Cross we're referring to was from a Serbian church, so we wanted to find out something about it because, to me, it's mind-blowing, it looks Norse.

A friend of a friend who was a Christian had a look at it. This is what he said:

> *"That's not a crucifixion cross at all. The lower arm is not long enough for Christ's legs. What is going on?" He said, "it is a representation of the Bible's version of our flat-earth."*

The square and stationary earth

Remember, wings are magnetic fields that include angels as well. Four angels on the four corners, the same as what we get. It tells us a lot, it's very informative. It reflects the cycles and seasons and solar year; the two equinoxes and the two solstices are covered in this.

Wings, described earlier, are an analogy for magnetic fields and the four angels are on the four corners and the North Pole is in the middle. Are they angels on the Serbian Cross? We looked at it for a long time because we knew there was something special about it.

The year of the Serbian Cross, by the way, which is very necessary, is the year i610. In mainstream years, that's 1610.

The Golden Ratio in the Sunflower Seeds

As most of you will know, the clue to the Golden Ratio is held in the sunflower. When you look at the patterns that the seeds make in the main head of the flower, you'll see what I mean.

Fibonacci's vortex
The two Fibonacci vortexes form a shape that can be thought of as a heart and also a C and a B.

You may notice this design on the tuning heads of violins, on top of Greco-Romano pillars, as well as the two laurel leaf branches. Even an owl's head, since their eyes seem to make the shape. So, if you put two Fibonacci's together, it creates what looks like an owl's eyes. Is this what the owl is all about all over the Middle Ages depictions? And is this why people who go to Bohemian Grove, worship the owl?

This is the double vortex that we live in, the flat plane. This is an antiquities depiction of the Luna cycle.

Still not convinced? I've said all along in architecture this was the double torus.

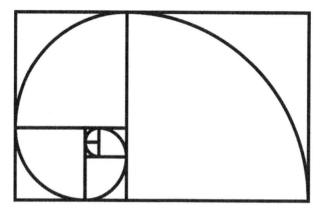

Fibonacci's Spiral Nicolás Damián Visceglio on Pixabay

The owl and the swastika
If you get two Fibonacci's and stand them upright –they look remarkably like an owl.

It gets tricky when we also find double spirals in the Mandelbrot fractals - the Mandelbrot Set, but it is all based on the same Golden Ratio.

Fractals
They are a joy to behold. They go deep, go in and in and in… and never seem to end.

The man who brought this to the mainstream was Arthur C. Clarke, the Sci-Fi writer. He only thought this up in the

1950s and it's odd that, now, only a few years later, they are considered to be a real thing.

Note: Arthur C. Clarke = C.C.

Fractal-art by Shabinh from Pixabay

The Mandelbrot Set

Though Mandelbrot studied his, now famous, 'Set' for about thirty years, he worked on them for about ten years. It took that long to understand it all and a decade to produce the software. So, to bring one image to the public's attention, it took about forty years of work. I think they are quite beautiful.

What I've found interesting is that the Mandelbrot's equations are depicted in paintings of the 1600s. I would like someone to explain why that is. Did they know, in that period, of his fractal equation? What has been found in a painting of the 17th Century is a fractal which can only mean that their understanding of this kind of science was profound.

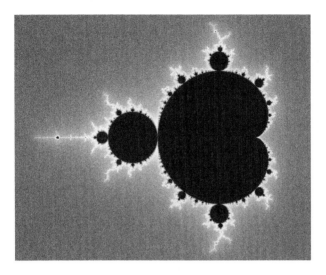

Mandelbrot Set by Skeeze on Pixabay

The Serbian Cross

If we now go back to the Serbian Cross at the beginning of this chapter, you'll find that it has four corners and the centre depicts the Mount Meru, which is a double vortex. The angels on the corners should be double vortexes. For the earth to exist, you need ten vortexes and this is exactly what the Serbian Cross shows you.

There are five double vortexes on the Serbian Cross from

the 1600s. Four are at the four corners of the earth, one at the North Pole, Mount Meru. Then the double vortex. If we consider we live on a plane between two torus fields, then there should be ten vortices – five above, five below. It is important to take this into account.

Remember, we learned that the first stable human cell had to have eight cells, like the cube. But, you must always keep a double vortex in the magnetic field, which can make a double torus field. There are eight and two, ten vortexes.

The decimal system
When you look carefully at an atom you see that it has ten electrons. This shows you two opposing clouds and then eight more on the second shell. That's ten as well. Also, our universe has ten vortexes.

> *Have you ever wondered why there has been a 'ten' numerical system? It's certainly not just a coincidence.*

This system represents the angels guarding the static square and stationary earth. Could this be the cause of the seasons that we experience on our earth?

Think of it this way, when you watch videos of the quantum levitator, which is a levitating disc, you'll see it has four vortexes – one on each corner. If you consider this to be similar to our earth, this could be the reason why the sun and the moon, literal luminaries that levitate constantly, move in a circle. The magnets of each 'angel' are moving

4 Sun Halo by Oimheidi on Pixabay

constantly, by being attracted to the next angel or magnet. Then it is attracted to the next angel/magnet and so on.

If you imagine this as an inertia flat plane, maybe four corners, or four magnets/angels, which has a magnet all the way around, then it would be magnetically pulled onto the next and then the next and the next and so on. This would drive our earth system, four corners and four angels through the flat plane.

Extra proof is the priceless image of a Sun Halo.

Sun halo

What you're witnessing when you see the image of the sun halo is magnetism. It's breathing in and out. The sun halo is an intense light or, more realistically, a gathering of lights. Therefore, even though it's a perfect circle when a halo appears you see four bright spots of light attracted by electromagnetism.

Is this force strong enough to attract, or even trap, sun rays or sunlight? Is there anything you can think of that could represent the four angels on the corner and a magnet in the middle? There is. It's called the Tesla Engine and the Tesla

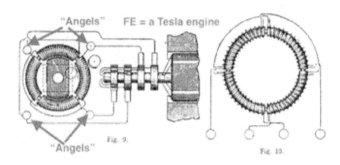

Flat Earth in Tesla's Engine

Engine is, coincidentally, a Flat Earth model.

Tesla and the Bible
In the Tesla engine, there is a magnet on each corner (representing the four angels, or angles if you like) above a square and stationary earth. As with the levitating moon and sun around the flat disc, the Tesla engine takes the current to the next magnet and the next magnet and so on.

So the Flat Earth model could be like the Tesla engine. Where did Tesla get his ideas from? I believe he got his ideas from the Holy Bible. I know, you're going to say to yourself…

*"No, man, he was a scientist! He thought
in scientific ways."*

Hold your horses for just a minute.

First, you have to consider Bishop Velimirovic. Velimirovic was Tesla's father and he was an Orthodox Priest who obviously read the Bible a lot. This is probably where Tesla got his ideas for his Engine. The Tesla Engine represented a square and stationary earth.

When you look at the map of the square and stationary earth, together with the angels and magnets we've just discussed, you'll see that the luminaries are moved on from one to the next. They move towards the centre and back out again – attracted by Mount Meru.

Now, you'll know that the angels we are aware of, have wings. Hold on to that thought as it will come in handy soon.

Tesla had an image in his head already, because his father most probably told him about the sun and the moon span above the earth. Tesla admitted that he never used mathematical equations when he created his models, but he did admit to having visions. He had seen things in his mind and a newspaper article stated exactly that:

"The miraculous vision of Nikola Tesla"

111

So, he never used mathematical equations. It was a vision that appeared to him, a mental image.

To have a vision of something, you would need to have seen it somewhere and that vision could be called from memories. From those, he would have worked it out. Tesla was really smart so the blueprints from the place where we live were put to work in his Tesla Engine.

The next bit of this you've probably not heard of before. I've been in Flat Earth movement since the get-go (2015), but Tesla's Engine provides us with overwhelming proof that our earth could be flat. I'd love to see globe-believing channels on YouTube pull that one apart.

There's another thing that proves we're on a flat earth. One from Mother Nature herself. The Cook Pine trees.

The Cook Pine Mystery
Cook Pine trees are very sensitive to electromagnetic fields and, in particular, to sunlight. The Cook Pines are found all over the world, in Sri Lanka, the USA and Australia. In Detroit, Motown city, people call them the 'Michael Jackson Tree'. Why? Because they lean.

Ken Thompson of the UK's Telegraph caught my attention (https://www.telegraph.co.uk/gardening/how-to-grow/ken-thompson-strange-leanings-cook-pine/) His article was titled: "The Strange Leanings of the Cook Pines" and he goes on to ask why they lean in such a way.

Here's a biggie: No scientist can work why the Cook Pine trees lean. It's a mystery, one that continues to baffle. But Flat Earthers know the answer!

Cook Pines always seem to point towards the Equator.

They even contort themselves to reach the equator - wherever they are. Scientists have validated this abnormality, but they just can't work out why this happens.

To find out the truth, let's look at the biggest fib of our age: the globe model.

If the globe model was a reality, and if the sun is ninety-three million miles away (which it's not, it's close by), then the oblique rays would come in at such an angle. It's not what we witness on the surface.

At the time of year, the images on my website were taken, the trees would not grow out that way at all. They wouldn't point towards the equator, they would point to the South. But they don't. So it must be false.

In reality, the Cook Pine trees leaning in that manner would only be possible on a flat plane.

It just makes no sense to the human brain - until you look at it on a flat earth projection with the sun's orbit in summer and the sun's equinoxes in winter. Even with this model in mind, if you wait six months, and then look at it, the sun would be on the other side and it would still make no sense. For this reason, it would be impossible for the leaning Cook Pines to point towards the apparent equator if it were on a globe.

The Roman Coliseum

This next idea was on Lee Mowat's video and I've also shown this myself. They are supposed to be sections of amphitheatres, viaducts or aqueducts. It seems like during the height of the Roman Empire, they needed thousands of tons of stone to carry water over very long distances. This makes absolutely no sense at all until you consider the Coliseums might be devices.

I've been to Rome myself, I've worked in another smaller amphitheatre when I was working as a Stonemason. The amphitheatres are quite unbelievable. Incredible.

Rome's Coliseum by Clarence Alford from Pixabay

The common consensus was that they were opened by Caesars, like Caligula in Rome, for Circus Maximus. Circuses were opened to keep the masses attention on sport, so they didn't think about the nightmare that was going on in their society. Much like we are brainwashed by television today.

The Roman leaders thought that with the minds of the masses virtually hypnotised, in a controlled state, they wouldn't be able to work things out with 'bread and circuses' going on around them to distract. It sounds like a good theory and there might be some truth in it.

Were the Coliseums always like that? Remember our earth has been reset, over and over. So, were they always just for people to go in and watch games? Let's have a little think.

CERN Switzerland by David Mark on Pixabay

In my spare time, I've been looking into free energy devices as it is my dream for everybody to someday have free energy. And you know what I've realised? The Coliseums were all about free energy. The Controllers had it then, they have it now, but they just don't want us to have it.

When I look at images of the CERN machine in Europe, it reminds me of the Coliseum. It blows cables in my head a bit. Basically, could Greco-Romano Coliseums be devices? If that's true, what could they be doing with them? Could you go into them to revitalise or recharge your body's orgon energy? Or could the devices be for levitating discs? Large discs for transporting people and materials.

The next bit is quite important in understanding where or what fasces tech is. Note, I don't say was, I say *is*.

There's a key here that, if you understand it, it could reveal this place can only be an inertia flat plane between two torus fields. By the end of this section, I'm hoping you'll find the weight of evidence will be overwhelming.

Controlling frequencies

The most important thing to understand is that people forget how to control frequencies. This is a really neat concept for me to explore because, in my spare time, I'm keen on building amplifiers.

This is how you can cancel out or increase the waveform. Because if you want to make sense of the fasces, which are magnetic rods which produce an ELM (electromagnetic) wave, the waves do not affect the target object. The reason is that they don't have the same frequency of energy and vibration as the object.

So, let's see how waves behave in general. It may look complicated, but it is really simple. This is the key, as it only comes in two forms.

With a wavelength you get amplitude. So, the wave can only have two things, the *frequency length*, which is calculated by the amount of time, in a second, that it goes up and down. And the bottom wavelength is its *strength*.

Now here comes the interesting stuff. If two wavelengths are sent out at the same moment, it's called phasing. They produce equal frequencies and the amplitude of the resulting wave will double.

People in the music industry know about this, which is why they use wooden and plastic resonance boxes for their speakers. It's the same frequency and it doubles the sound. The better the box, the better the sound.

magnetic field strength

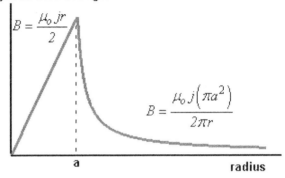

Ampere's Law - Magnetic Field Density Chart

Magnetic density charge

In the magnetic force density related chart, another piece of the puzzle has been found. You would think that the scientific symbol for Magnetic Density, would be D (for Density), but it's not. What represents it, is a B. Also, you'd think an F would represent Force. You'd think. But an H is used instead.

So, what's going on here then? It's a bit unusual you must admit. Unless you consider this question:

"What does the HB mean?"

The H is an anagram for the fasces. The arrows, the shape of arrows, the path to the North Pole. Or the Holy Grail cup. The B is a spiralling vortex. I explained this by mentioning the biggest bands the world has ever known, bands like ABBA and BB King etc. It just goes on and on and on.

HB, isn't that a coincidence? Not.

Understanding Fasces

Two identical waves 180 degrees out of phase will completely cancel each other out in the process. It's called *phase cancellation* or *destructive interference*. This is important and I'll explain why.

If you want the knowledge of waves to be useful, to make fasces weapons we have to understand *natural vibrational frequency*.

Atoms in sandstone, cement or brick can project a beam. So, if you project a beam with the same vibration as say, sandstone, what will happen? If you leave it long enough, the strength or amplitude, of the electromagnetic force will create holes. The atoms will vibrate violently, they will heat up and, finally, the stone will fall apart into dust. Does this ring a bell?

Microwaves

The same thing happens in the house when you put coffee in your microwave. I'm not just talking about warming it up, I'm talking about if you left coffee in the microwave long enough it would turn into water and disappear.

*So, you could have a miniature fasces
device in your kitchen as a microwave oven
is a fasces!*

What happens when you project two waves at the same frequency, at the same amplitude? Waves that are not sent out at the same time, but exactly half the frequency length. Cancellation. They cancel each other out.

I know, fasces technology seems bleak, but there's always a bright side, which is epic, and I always like to talk about that.

Double or quits

Since gravity, or electromagnetic acceleration, are two vortex waves opposing magnetic fields, the moment they have the same strength, they cancel each other out. This is one of the biggest reasons why we can only possibly live on a flat and stationary plane. But also, we need to have two opposing torus fields, not just the one.

As above, so below.

The proof that there are two, is the amplitude that I've just explained. You send out half a wavelength less and it will cancel out. This is what is happening here. It's perfect.

The amplitude of one is bigger than the opposing force and

it will go up and down. If we were taught this fact in our educational systems, we would know that we could only be living on a flat plane. Sadly, we're all kept ignorant.

Now, you can either double the wave of magnets or you can put them together and cancel them out. You can even levitate devices as I mentioned before, with the quantum levitator.

All this knowledge has been there all along, it's just being rediscovered. Everything I'm revealing to you now is not in the realm of fantasy, but reality. This earth can only exist as a flat plane between two magnetic vortexes in a toroidal field.

What have we learned?
We've learned that there are possibly magnets, or angels, or magnetic forces on the four corners of this realm. This possibly being the cause of the seasons, the discs or the luminaries (Sun and Moon) are attracted to the one angel, or magnet, and then on to the next and the next, back round to the magnet in the middle of the seasons and then back around again. Just like the square and stationary earth.

And coincidence, the Tesla machine happens to be the same model. So, we are more or less living in a Tesla-like machine and this is where Tesla got the tech.

Then we looked at something that has never been looked at before (not while I've been on the scene anyway), and that's the leaning Cook Pine tree mystery. This proves, beyond a shadow of a doubt that if they are all pointing at the equator and the sun is supposed to be ninety-three million miles away – this is an impossibility. The only way it works is if it's a flat plane projection.

I then explained how the fasces work, which is very similar to the microwave technology in your kitchen.

I also mentioned that wavelengths can be amped-up or cancelled out. Amped-up, in fasces technology, means things will turn to dust. All you need to do is find the frequency of, say, a bottle, or glass, and match it with the same frequency (opera singers can do it with the tone of their voice), and the glass will shatter. When you do find the same frequency, the atoms will vibrate violently. They will heat up, fall apart, de-aggregate and then turn to dust. That's the bad side of fasces. Ramped-up exponential. But the good thing is it can be cancelled out which is what is happening on our flat plane.

Did all of that go in? You may need to go over it again. The next chapter is going to get a bit crazy, so you'll need to hold on to your horses.

.

.

8 THE HOLY GRAIL

Why would scientists for all these hundreds of years, tell us the earth is round when it's flat? Where is the point in it?

Crescent Park

Remember the Star Garden, Crescent Park in Sydney? This park has been designed cleverly as something is going on with the design. It's a flat earth map, the azimuthal equidistant, a beautiful geometrical layout. And then, mind blow, it shows Technasma waves. How could they have known? They've only just discovered Technasma waves. It just goes to prove that the designer of that garden knew all about it all along.

Now, in the image the follows, you'll see that designer seems to have strangely aligned his garden pattern to the left, and I honestly can't establish why that's been done. It might be because it's the course of the stars over our flat plane under this electromagnetic roof, or he knew something we don't. Perhaps you know? But, one thing that becomes apparent, while examining this park, is the name of it: Crescent. Crescent means *growing*. Not just growing but growing fractally.

We noticed one thing in that Crescent garden, that there appears to be a large tower in the middle. So, could that be Mount Meru? Or perhaps the Tower of Babel?

Star Garden, Crescent Park, Sydney

Mount Meru, or the vortex torus, is also known as the Tower of Babel. Remember, it's got a spiral going up it, but it seems extremely high compared to the size of the earth that is represented by the design. Did that Australian park designer want to tell people that it touches the dome and it could be the highest point of our tent, below a canopy of stars? We know that the garden maps out Technasma waves. That designer knew something.

The Phoenix

So, when you look up images of the Tower of Babel, it looks unfinished to my eyes. And on the top, there's an open-winged phoenix. The phoenix analogy is that it rises from the flames or 'resurgi' - resurgence. But we know that an animal in antiquity with its wings opened means, what?

Magnetic fields.

We also spotted in it, for some strange reason, the reference of the fish. The fish, as you probably know, is connected to Christianity, Christ and the rest. But the fish, 'vesica piscis', is actually in the Technasma waves and it's on so many depictions through antiquity.

The fish shows up next to the toroidal, which could be a course of stars or something. The Mount itself could even be associated, or have something to do with, the North Pole star. It could even sustain it. How do we know?

On the top of the unfinished Tower of Babel, there's a lovely phoenix. Most of these towers seem unfinished, have you ever seen a finished Tower of Babel? Or Meru. I guess it just symbolises the regeneration. Or it's just another winged animal that's showing us that it's the centre of the magnetic universe.

You guessed right. It is. The designer of this park knows how this place works. It's crazy, but he's not the only one.

We've established that Tesla based his Engine on basically the square and stationary earth with knowledge from the Bible - the four angels or the four magnets on the four corners. I'll explain how that works.

You need ten vortexes; two, one on each angel (angle) and two in the middle, the two vortexes at Mount Meru. It's a ten-vortex system

Now I've explained how wave acceleration works, with stacking or nesting neatly in pyramids, but the designer of the park has made Mount Meru. He has presented the same amount of torus fields in this small device.

Now, there's a guy on YouTube called Super Magnet Guy and he has a device that can produce 10,000 gauss or the reading for magnetism. 10,000 is an awful lot of power. He has got eight angels (or angles), eight magnets, two for each angle for it to work. Think of the atom.

Since magnetism is always in two-directions and nests in corners or angles, maybe I should say four angels. So, what he has done is he's got the opposing polarities cancelling out onto the next, which makes a total of four angels. So, I've shown how Mount Meru works.

How could he know this? This guy has done the same as Tesla and many others who seem to know what this earth is. This is reality. This is how it all works. It's crazy stuff.

Symbology in Logos
I would like you to Google the 'Mixed Martial Arts' logo. It's from Dallas, the Kung Fu people, the Martial Arts people. Examine it. Do you see anything in it? It is a hexagon, but there's more.

In the depiction of the Gettysburg Anniversary coin that follows, on one side you get the fasces in the middle with the Labrys, which I told you is a moon calendar. But it's more than a moon calendar. It has two opposing phases, thirteen days of the new waxing moon versus the thirteen days of the waning dark moon. This is what the Labrys does.

Gettysburg Battle Anniversary coin, 1936

So you have the Labrys which tells you what's happening on the solar calendar. Interestingly, this labrys has been adopted by the lesbian pride movement because it's associated with the female cycle. And you have the fasces, which is an energy weapon, a sonic energy weapon, with three crosses, the bonds, to hold it together.

These crosses, you'll see all over antiquity. What you don't get with these vortices type scenarios are straight lines. Why? Because there are no straight lines in nature. As you saw in the Crescent Park in Sydney with the Technasma lines. This is how they are. This is why the sun won't go in a straight line but will always arc over us.

Now if you put two men in a CERN device, which looks like a Coliseum, the two opposing vortexes, opposites, will constantly recycle. There's a constant recycling battle going on.

If you go back to the Mixed Martial Arts logo, you'll find they have a pyramid, Mount Meru, inside the Labrys and the fasces inside the octagon. The person who designed this 100% knows.

The X Code

You will see the X Code everywhere in antiquity as it's a reference to the fasces. It is also on an emblem on the city of Amsterdam's coat of arms. The three bindings, or the three bonds, of the fasces and then, down below, it will show you a J or a 762. You have 762 and you let two fasces and there's one behind there as well. The three Xs in a row represents the fasces in antiquity.

The Maltese Cross

The Maltese cross is a ten-pointed star, like our cube, or like our ten-vortex system. It's got the Fleur de Lys opposing vortexes. It even has the four angels on the Maltese Cross. But more, in many depictions of the Maltese Cross, a dove is flying downwards. But doves have never been known to fly down like that, they're not dive-bombers. So, what's going on?

It's over Mount Meru. It's over the North Pole hole and it's flying downwards. What's happening is that the dove represents the natural light of the sun. The light from the sun has been magnetised and it gets sucked back down the North Pole hole and back into the torus system where it is decompressed again on the other side following the magnetic fields torus path as we see here. So, it goes through Mount Meru.

Mount Meru is a pyramid which is believed to be artificial and there's another pyramid below, which is the South Pole. We believe it to be twelve kilometres below Mount Meru.

Seasonal luminaries

Mount Meru is a double-sided pyramid. Think back to the nesting, or stacking, and you'll understand that this thing is active and it's giving off high frequencies. It is dictating seasons by drawing in the luminaries of the sun and the moon which are levitating from magnet to magnet with the four angels on each corner. Then they move steadily back to the centre, to Mount Meru, and then back out again dictating our seasons.

Magnetised light

So, it's sucked down into the beautiful light of Mount Meru. Do you know what light is called when it's magnetised? Fasces, which means, Fazer and it's a light Fazer. A light Fazer is a laser.

When the light of the dove emanates through the North Pole hole, we get laser lights of the Northern lights which we know as the Aurora Borealis.

Now there are so many examples of everyday fasces in use in our reality, it's quite mind-blowing when you know what we are seeing. It's magnetised light, and this is how industry uses the magnetised light in the modern-day. There are fasces in the modern world right now.

You'll see fasces in laser printers. In the middle section, you will see cylindrical magnets so what you have in there are three magnets that are bound with a ribbon holding them together. This is a fasces device and everyday use of a fasces. Have you ever seen that black box when you got to the disco-tech? It's inside that.

A Laser Device

Only printers, CDs and DVDs have these lasers, so they are fasces, magnetised light, and they point it in spectrums or mirrors, or spinning lenses, to create that effect.

Unbelievably, there are small hand-held fasces you can have

around your home. That's what they were using in antiquity and we're still using them now. It's your conventional everyday laser. And, this is a shocker, it's not very expensive. They're on sale for about $50 in Japan.

Laser light is a target laser and a taser. That's what's happening as well.

"The future of professionals and citizen defence"

You can have your own little fasces and it's a targeting laser. It's insane.

So, we're going to move on now as we're going to do some more decoding. But we'll reflect on what we've learned, as I said, this takes some, not so much understanding, I think it's quite simple, but it does take some spiritual processing. That's why I've left it until now for you to chew it over. I'm doing my best to try and explain these subjects. To me, it's very important.

The Holy Grail
There are two ways of looking this, side on – a W structure or looking down a twisted X. This X you will see all over antiquity. We're going to look at some ideas. They don't ever show you the side view of this system, so I'll go through a few. You'll probably work it out for yourself.

There are images on my website of an Ethiopian church that has the Fleur de Lys pointing in. It's all in plain sight.

Again, all the images represent Mount Meru, four angels, from the Ethiopian church. It's also on the Catholic papal cross. You have all the elements I've explained before the four angels, Mount Meru, the inertia flat plane. They really can't help themselves.

The P

But the P, what is the P? It is called Pyron, Pyro, and that's the meaning of the word giro, which means ring or circle. So, what they've done is they've told you, with the P, that this is a ring or a circle, that the system is an inertia flat plane. And, yet again, there's a cross-section with the four angels and the four corners. It's crazy. The Catholic Church knows!

The Catholic Papal Cross

You may remember an advert for Microsoft where a dog was looking for Windows XP. It was taken away in 2014, but what was the XP all about? It was the XP for the system we live in. Getting convinced yet?

The fish shows up again and again in ancient depictions. They all reveal the whole system we're living on, in plain sight. From magnet to magnet back to middle and back out again. Everything covered in that beautiful system.

The Skull and Crossbones by Clker-Free-Vector-Images from Pixabay

The skull and crossbones

Skull and crossbones, just like the Pirates. X marks the spot alright. It really does. On a pirate map. It's all starting to make perfect sense, isn't it!

What about St. Peter's Square? When you take the time to look at it, it's not a square, it's a circle. And what they show you with that design is the flat earth. There's the cross, the four angles on each corner and it even tells you of the summer solstice and winter solstice, and the equinoxes.

St. Peter's Square the Basilica by Heinz Teuber from Pixabay

There's a shadow that casts off the obelisk at different times of the year which has been long established as a calendar. But it also represents our flat earth system perfectly. This is all over antiquity and there's no escaping it.

The X code is our system

Even Osiris has to do the X code. This X code is everywhere. Once you see it, you won't un-see it. It's in old Mayan depiction, just like the cross of St. Andrews on the Scottish flag. The cross of St. Andrews was, apparently, a crucifixion of the opposite way around. They've even got the Phoenix with the wings open - magnetised.

We have some Masonic 5th degree and 6th-degree awards. It is St. Andrews cross, but it's in green. I don't know why maybe it's the Celtic colour. But the X is in there again. Then we have the Labrys, and the double pyramid and the G. This all goes right through our culture.

Alistair Crowley and Egypt

I'm sure you know all about Alistair Crowley. Anything associated with Egypt is associated with this guy and he's all over popular culture. He's depicted in an image with the X code, and he's telling you what this place is.

The Christian Cross

There's a photograph of Diago Maradona, the Argentinian footballer, displaying the 'hands of God goal'. He's looking up and pretending he gives a shit when he's just the worst Capitalist on earth. In any interview you watch him in, he's always doing the sign of the cross, not the Christian cross though.

The Beatles

St. Pepper's Lonely Hearts Club Band. It's on the album cover. All over it. It's all in plain sight. Take a look at the original picture and you'll see there are the crosses, Mount Meru, and our inertia flat plane – the one above, and the one below. Both pyramids are facing in. Their album cover just screams at us what this place is and it's on one of the most important covers of contemporary music history. Even Alistair Crowley makes an appearance on it. That album cover shows us the place where we live there's no avoiding it. When you look at it, all will become clear and you're going to see it all the time.

The X Factor

Did they actually sit around a table and think that title up? When they were initialising these talent shows, why did they refer to it as the X factor? If you have talent, you've got the X factor? Who decided that? They're showing you.

This is everywhere in popular culture and you can find it anywhere in antiquity as well.

The X code is in the Vatican symbol, and in the Grand Orange Lodge of Scotland. The Grand Orange Lodge of Scotland is Masonic, but they have thistles instead of the laurel leaves. You'll see that the laurel leaves are two opposing vortexes. In the case of the symbol used by the Orange Lodge, they've used thistles of two opposing vortexes and then there's a star in the middle and the cross.

The Crossed Keys of the Vatican by Clker-Free-Vector-Images from Pixabay

The keys of the Vatican in a cross

You'll have missed this one, no doubt, so much that you're probably going to be rifling through your own images. It's on an Egyptian ring – the being, or entity, has her wings opened up in the shape of a cross. What it represents is the magnetic torus fields of Technasma – it's incredible.

Zeus' lightning bolt

This is often talked about in our flat earth community, it's a symbol of an electrical charge and it's depicted in a cross shape and on a sort of speaker. Do you think this is by accident?

A lot of thought has gone into the designs so they're showing everything in plain sight. It's for the initiated, the ones who know (which is you now, because I'm telling you). For some reason, they're giving away their secrets and it's a pleasure to explore all of this.

Double phoenixes in images show that they are Magnetised. The double pillars, which have the binding around them, will make them magnetised. The whole whammy, all in one go, our flat plane.

The sign of the goat

Also, the evil goat, there's some reverence with these people. I don't think the goat himself is a bad critter, but his horns represent two pronounced double vortexes. Even the Welsh Guard's main emblem is a goat. They take that goat to every single event they do - double vortexes.

It's incredible, isn't it?

9 AXIS MUNDI

As you saw in an earlier chapter of this book, most people recognise the swastika, but what we never see is the side view. We're always given images that look down on the vortex system. So, what we're going to do now is highlight a few things that will drive this home the way you never would have expected. The way that this reality is encoded.

On my website, you'll see over a 1,000 of these images that prove the incredible secrets that are encoded in our reality. Don't worry, I'll just overwhelm you at just how much this is in your reality. Not to shock you, but just to show you that it is everywhere.

Once you know, it is overwhelming, and you'll probably just read this and think

"Oh Wow! Yeah, of course!"

The way I did.

Clocks

It seems everything is encoded in all our reality. I will give you some examples from our known history to drive home that the controllers, the elites (who are the Phoenicians), the powers that should *not* be, know what this place is. A massive clue turned up one day and it blew my socks off. This is just about best intrigue you've ever imagined.

Now, the '1' (one), you will always see the '1', remember the numerical system is based on this. The '1' is the Axis Mundi or the World Tree, the axis between four angels and our inertia flat plane. It's on the American dollar, it's everywhere, but the one place you would not expect to see it is on your everyday clock or watch.

If you take a look at the pattern and the way it's been set-up, the reason for this is because of Tesla's Vortex map. There is a code, a circle, called Tesla's (or the Gurdjieff) Circle. Or the Rodin, it's a vortex map. You can look them up on YouTube. Really fine stuff. They are about vortex physics or vector physics.

What you get is a circle, which is a nine-pointed star but, of course, it's got the Axis Mundi. It's also got the four corners, and all the other stuff we've talked about throughout this book. You can even see the nine-pointed star represented on a clock's face.

Gurdjieff is one of the greatest minds of our day. He was a bit of a Tesla-type. He seems a pretty friendly guy and, by the way, he has an excellent view on reality. Look him up on Google.

The Tesla Code

So, there's this code, and it's called the Tesla Code. It is mind-blowingly amazing. Because I can't put a video in a book (yet), you'll have to look it up on YouTube or go to my channel and you'll see it there. As you watch the video, keep an eye on the blue triangle. Now, what you will see is that it will go 6, 9, 3 - or the other way, 3, 9, 6. It will repeat this pattern into eternity. Forever and ever and ever. It's just incredible. Right?

What it is, is the opposing torus fields, the double torus fields, but it goes on into infinity. Both ways. When you take a close look at the clock, you'll see there are the four torus fields. Now, this map of Tesla's Code, and Mark Rodin's Code and Gurdjieff's Code, is this, simply multiplying each number by two. That's it.

- You get 1, 2, 4, 8, 16. But the 16 is always represented by a 7, their reason in this map
- 1 add 6 = 7 etc. That was the circle with the nine-pointed star

On the four magnets, you get the 3, 6 and the 9. Right? Ok. It works on the eternity loop, both clockwise and anti-clockwise. Not only that, but this also fits perfectly with the flat earth as the Azimuthal Equidistant. It accurately presents both double torus with an inertia flat plane.

Reverse engineered?
Clocks can go in reverse? Is there any evidence for this? In antiquity, the Jewish people used to have clocks that went in reverse. There are not very many of them as, in modern days, they have to go clockwise.

Now, there is a counter-clockwise clock and it is in Prague, on a synagogue. It was kind of them to let us know that clocks are so much more than we've been told. I couldn't get an image of this for the book, so you'll need to look it up on Google or my website, and you'll find it there.

Right now, I'm going to drive home to you that this accurately shows the model using Tesla Code and a mathematical theorem. All of it:

- Axis Mundi
- Flat plane
- Torus fields
- Magnets
- Four angels on the four corners

All of this evidence is on our clocks. They most certainly knew about it in antiquity. Who of them invented it, I couldn't quite say, but it is amazing. Now we know what this place is and what the shape is, let's decode some more of our reality. For many of the images, you'll need to check out my website or my YouTube channel.

There is an ancient Sumerian image I must have shown a hundred times on my Flat Earth British YouTube channel, and what you've always thought was an electrical device, well, it's a damn sight more than that. It's an accurate representation of our flat earth plane.

It's the Axis Mundi in the middle and the four corners.

Number 8

Now let's take a look at the numbers 1 (one) through to 8 (eight). The 8 is everywhere in antiquity. If you look at the Maltese Cross, they give you some sort of flowers to show you where the torus fields are and you get the numbers 1 through to 8. Remember, two torus per angel, per magnet, North and South Pole. This applies in each luminary, the moon and the sun, onto the next, and then back into the centre, through the centre pyramid, which is a double pyramid because it goes underground as well, to the South Pole, and dictates our seasons.

The Maltese Cross

Every single aspect of it works. If you don't get it after this, I just don't know what else to say. It's all there. All of it. There are so many clues it is hard to put into words. But it's more than that. It has something to do with the colours too.

Red, White and Blue

First the white represents the sunlight, and then you get the red and the blue, and what these colours determine is the double vortex. They're showing you the vortex, the four double vortexes. In the number 8 (eight), there's the Axis Mundi, the inertia flat plane, then the blue and red colours represent the double torus.

How many flags of the world have got red, white and blue in them? Can you think of any? It's right there. All in plain sight.

It is on the top of the Indian Cross which is, again, our flat plane, the Axis Mundi, the ring around it has 1 (one) through to 8 (eight), like our cube. Then the two vortexes per angel.

The Ark of the Covenant

Now it's obvious to many people know that the Ark of the Covenant is a device. What the people are carrying around is some large battery with an electrical device on top, a conduit. In the battery, you get positive and negative terminals on the top. It is so obvious this is a device.

They are two opposing torus fields. As in the I Ching, the Chinese diagram, the serpents, or the dragons or snakes. They all show you the 8 (eight).

The Cross Code

I'm from Wales and there are so many Celtic Crosses everywhere in my country. These crosses show you the vortexes, the four angels, on each corner and in the middle. The Axis Mundi, Mount Meru, all these are depicted on every Celtic Cross.

Buddhists represent the lotus flower in the middle of their

cross, and this shows you the double vortex. It's got the arrows coming out.

Christian Cross

Take a look at the Christian Cross, you have an eight-cube structure inside of a lotus flower. In the middle, you've got the flower of life. You can see now that they know about the stable eight on the Christian Cross. I've yet to establish why the bottom bit is longer but, these crosses tell you everything about the cube and everything from the beginning, and they tell you this to ensure that they have explained exactly how this plane works. From the bottom up.

Flower of Life by Nicolás Damián Visceglio on Pixabay

Flower of Life

So, the flower of life is in the middle and the Technasma waves coming out are interpreted as a lotus flower. The arrows are facing out on the four corners and the inertia flat plane is between.

Just a thought, remember that Crescent Park, with the Technasma waves? I was puzzled as to why it was all sort of skewed to the right. With the Technasma waves, I'm sort of wondering if this is the same thing.

The Red Rose

This is self-explanatory actually. The symbol of the Red Rose is another shape of the Christian Cross, but it's got absolutely everything in it. The intertwining snakes around the column. They are charging or causing a magnetic field. The Axis Mundi would be the Tudor flower or the Delacroix flower.

The Cross of Constantine

Look up the Cross of Constantine. That's the flag for the Isle of Wight in the UK. Again, the P in the cross is there to tell you it's a circle.

The Indian wheel

How many prongs are there in the Indian wheel? 1 (one) through 8 (eight). Like our stable eight-cell, our Axis Mundi, the cross-code. Every single thing we've explored in this book is in the Indian wheel. It is an accurate representation of the place where we live – a double vortex system.

The Romany coin

On Romany gypsy coins, there is a symbol from the Middle Ages, used around i500 (I mean 1500). During this era, there was a saying for the Roman soldiers, they used to say "Roma!" but it was sort of a counter code, a word that has survived amongst the Romany people. By the way, they are not gypsy people, they are Romanies. Their sign is the same, the B, or the two opposing vortexes, and Axis Mundi and our inertia flat plane between.

The Buddhist Mandala

I've got a beautiful antique Buddhist Mandala on my wall. But again, it shows the middle, our Mount Meru, and the four corners, where the four angels even on that depiction. This is in every single culture, everywhere, on all logos, our popular culture, music, maps, everything. It's true.

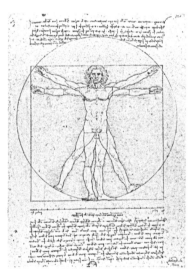

Michael Angelo's Man

Michael Angelo's man

Very famous, the exhibitionist, how many limbs are you

seeing here? Arms and legs. Yes, eight.

The Vatican Square
Again, as we've already established it's not a square, it's a circle and it shows us the inertia flat plane, the Axis Mundi, and the four angels on the four corners.

The UN Flag
As we saw in a previous chapter, yes, the UN flag is divided into 33 subsections. It's two opposing vortexes. Each section is divided into 33 subsections and the two opposing vortexes are the laurel leaves.

The Starbucks Logo
Check out the Starbucks logo and you'll find it all over antiquity. The Melusine is a double-tailed female Goddess. What you get are two tails which represent two opposing vortexes.

The Society of Christ
Nearly all Flat Earthers recognise the Society of Christ symbol used by the Jesuits or, the Society of Christ, the Secret Service, the police force and enforcers for the Vatican.

It has the H & H, well that's two opposing vortexes. They have an X in the middle (cross), so you know where Mount Meru is. The I is Mount Meru, and S is the snake of the dragon. But how many shiny stars or shiny things, sun rays can you see? Eight longer sun rays.

Coat of Arms (logo) The Society of Christ

The Mappa Mundi

The Mappa Mundi is an ancient flat earth map. I've seen a few different versions of the Mappa Mundi. The Hereford Mappa Mundi shows you the four corners and this is the same thing that shows you the inertia flat plane and square and stationary earth. It's by Prof Orlando Ferguson, 1893, with the four angles in place.

The Michael Angelo design by Giovanni d' Fiorentini, of Rome is the same thing as it shows four angels, four corners, the Mount Meru, Axis Mundi, and the inertia flat plane. It's depicted on a good few buildings, that show you on our flat model.

Church Dome inside the Vatican by Manfred Neidel from Pixabay

The Vatican's Domed Ceiling

On the following page, you'll see an image of the domed ceiling inside the Vatican. It is the same again. Eight angels, you have the circle inside, the inertia flat plane.

Jesus Christ

When you look at the images of Jesus Christ on the Cross or at images where he's going walkabout, you'll see a star, or shine, a halo, in the background behind his head. It's a depiction of the disc. How many sections are there? Eight. Think there' something in that?

By the way, the Indian cross shows you the swastika in the middle. As I explained earlier, that's the way the toroidal system looks like when you're looking down from above.

Incidentally, I've got a tattoo on my arm that I got done when I was eleven years of age and it is 100% identical to

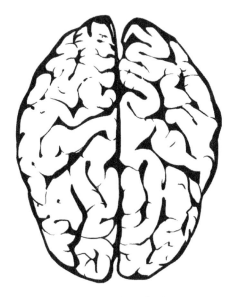

The Human Brain by Colleen O'Dell from Pixabay

the image on the Byzantium coin. What are the chances? On the Byzantium coin from 1143-1118 BC, you'll see it's got the orb and sceptre, and this is the inertia flat plane.

The human heart and brain

Does the human heart remind you of anything? There are eight chambers, the same as the eight-sided cube, the same as the eight vortexes on each corner. Also, when you look at images of the human brain, you get the same kind of thing again. Just like the angel – two opposing vortexes on a slice of the human brain on a CT scan.

Ok, so what does the double helix show you? Two opposing torus fields, and a centre bit.

Italy's Coat of Arms by Clker-Free-Vector-Images from Pixabay

What about the four-leaf clover? Do you ever wonder why you feel so lucky when you find one? It's the two double vortexes, the two torus fields.

Coats of Arms

On some Coat of Arms or logos, you'll normally see two opposing torus fields, or a bird with his wings open, showing you that it is magnetised. This indicates they are producing 'order out of chaos', chaos meaning it's not magnetised. Order meaning all the atoms have been aligned and are now magnetised.

If you go to a battle re-enactment, you'll probably see

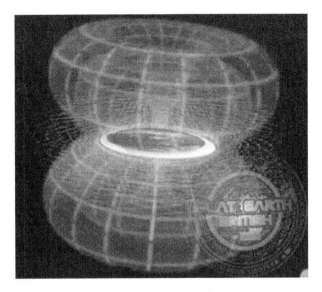

The Double Torus Field

Roman soldiers. Take a look at their shields. Apparently from antiquity, it is incredible why they need the bar through the middle. The whole thing is in there. You have our inertia flat plane, the Axis Mundi, four torus fields, as well, the angels on each corner.

Ok now, going through the North Pole hole. It shows you how rays pass through a magnetic ring.

The image that follows shows you the double torus of our universe. It can't be any other way. The way that I've explained it in this book.

So that's what it looks like. If you're on a flat plane, down here on the inertia flat plane there is a dome, as such, as an electromagnetic – that's their Van Allen Belt that they can't pass through.

The Union Flag

And then you have the British flag or the Union flag as its proper name. It is the same, two opposing torus's, Axis Mundi, and our inertia flat plane.

The World Cup.

Now, 1930 to 1970, this first World Cup here was used. It was invented by a guy called Jules Rimmer and it was a beautiful trophy called the *Jules Rimmer Trophy*. It had wings which were opened, which means it's magnetising. Again, it had the octagon, the eight-sided cube.

In 1974, the Globalists got hold of this and they got rid of the *Jules Rimmer Trophy* because it was showing you too much of the place where we live. They stuck a globe on it.

So, since 1974, when the footballers win this, the players spin around the globe in spirals and never really recognise what's going on or know it's true meaning. Or maybe some of the elites do - who knows?

~+~

Since the beginning of this book and my video series on YouTube, we have been learning the true meaning of a lot of stuff, wouldn't you say?

What I've explained to you is that your everyday watch shows you a double-sided vortex and it shows you that clocks were, in antiquity, that the vortex can work in reverse as well. It's on an infinite looping style that I explained to you, from Tesla Code with 3,6,9.

And then I explained that we could prove, beyond a shadow of a doubt, that the elites know what this place is.

Welcome to the place where you live!

Now, all that's left is for me to show you an example of a city that reveals exactly what has happened in antiquity and how the town planners coped with creating something out of nothing. We're going to take a look at Amsterdam.

The British Union Flag by Pete Linforth from Pixabay

10 THE SECRETS IN AMSTERDAM

Looking into the secret of Amsterdam, if you're into Star Forts and mud floods, this will make a lot of sense. Plus, it's the most persuasive case I've seen yet. In the previous Chapter, concerning Aquatec and water, we've learned that we can:

- store it
- purify it
- desalinate it in times of drought
- used magnetic vitalisation
- and use steam heating for buildings

Now, let's change the scenario a bit. What if there was a flood or a mud flood? How would you protect your city? If you'd like to see images and videos of Amsterdam, you should go check out my YouTube videos so that you can see what I'm talking about.

Amsterdam

The most famous dam of all, Amster*dam*. If you're going to be protecting your city, would you build a wall with vertical lines? No. That won't work too well. The best way to do it would be to build it like a dam is built.

Now, a dam has a stepping type structure. The steps are

not steps for people to walk on. But they are step-structures made to divert water, to direct the water flow downwards. This way it causes the water to lose connective energy so that it doesn't jump over the dam, which it would if it was just a smooth wall and didn't have steps. The type of design I'm describing here is used for the prevention of floods.

In older Victorian dams, they created them the same way, as a sort of steppingstone structure. Some have holes where water can pass through and some are particularly enormous - think of the Boulder Dam in the USA and you'll be along the right lines.

Amphitheatre vs Dam

Are the Amphitheatres, or Roman Coliseums, damns? If you think about it carefully, would a whole theatrical company cart itself off to the desert just to find some remote amphitheatre to perform a concert? It doesn't seem particularly likely.

As I believe it, Amphitheatres are a type of ancient dam. They've got the stepping structures in the shape, style and form of audience seating areas. If you're having a hard time getting your mind wrapped around this idea, think of it this way: A damn becomes obsolete when a river dries up, but the local population would return to that same gathering place to use it for something else.

Amphitheatres have always had two uses. All is revealed when you break the word up and you find it has two meanings:

- When there's water in it, it's a water tank –
  Amphi- (or amphibious)
- When there's no water in it, the same place
  can be used as a theatre

What else do they mean by two uses?

From antiquity, we get what you know now as an ancient
dam - or an amphitheatre - in the mud. Amsterdam isn't
the only city in Holland with a 'dam' in the name. My
favourite city where I had the best Christmas ever, was
Rotter*dam*. There's also:

- E*dam*
- Monacun*dam*
- Svesen*dam*
- Masa*dam*
- Alblasser*dam*
- Apalege*dam*

It just goes on and on.

Canal systems

You have the centrum where there are strange canal
systems all around the city. Go research the history of this.
On my website, you'll see we've dug out a few old maps,
but here we'll go over what we have unearthed.

Many of the ancient maps of Amsterdam depict the Star

159

Fort. Amsterdam is much bigger than it was then, so right now we'll focus on the old parts, its canals and its Star Fort.

In my YouTube video about Amsterdam, you'll see a map from 1700 (or what we are led to believe is the 1700s), and it's Amsterdam. You might recognise that the map that is depicted there is upside down as many maps were in those days. It is North and South, reversed. The only reason for this, I can guess, is that that was just the way the sailors saw it when they entered the port, so they portrayed it like that in their maps.

Let's start from the beginning and try to work this out.

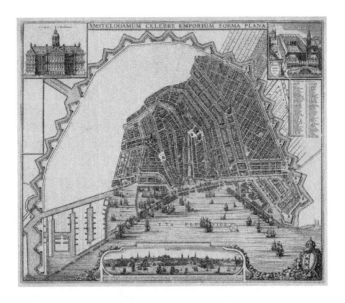

Imprint-Card-Visscher, Amsterdam

To find out how Amsterdam grew, we have look at the oldest map. Just bear in mind that maps are not conclusive, but we have to go with what we've got and the oldest map of Amsterdam available today, was dated i538 (the year 1538). Then, had a great canal going into the city.

There is something very startling concerning the new city, something that's not logical. When you look at that map, you have to ask where does the canal lead to? In the map, the big Grand Canal leads to nowhere. Why did the architects do that?

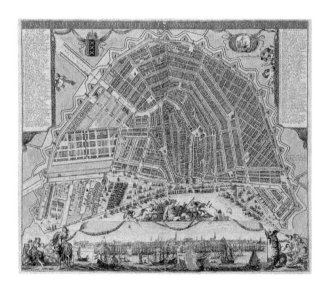

Amsterdam 1688

*Because the designer of Amsterdam
already knew what the final shape would
be.*

How on earth did they know how to lay it out, centuries before? It is a puzzle. If you go all the way around, they seem to have known what was going to be there in the future. So that was great foresight from the designers of the planners of Amsterdam city centrum, don't you think?

There is another map, from the 1700s and, in it, you will see the canal systems which, again, are going nowhere. Nothing else seems to be happening outside of the centrum.

We can even jump to another century later, and to another continent, to America. In my YouTube videos on Flat Earth British, I have shown thousands of images and they all show a 'future' layout, one that's already established. But, the really odd thing about them is that there are no people there.

I'm filled with questions like, how would they know? Is it planning, or not? What's the official narrative for Amsterdam planning? If you visit a website called www.Amsterdam.info, you'll see it says the following:

*"History of Amsterdam. Amsterdam, the
greatest planned city of northern Europe."*

Why on earth would they start a city, go inwards with a straight canal tilt it at an angle and go precisely nowhere? They already knew, in advance, that it would take six angles to complete a circle at the centre.

Ancient historians tell you that, in the beginning, the area where Amsterdam was built, was a desolate swampland. There was no civilisation, no population of people, at all. It was just a simple swampy paradise occupied by birds and beavers.

Incidentally, Amsterdam is shaped like a beaver's head. Is it just a coincidence that the swampy area was the first piece of Amsterdam in the shape of a beaver's head? A piece of land that originally looked like a farmer's field with a canal running through it, with tens of thousands of beavers in it.

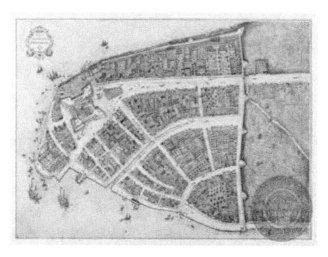

Amsterdam, shaped like a Beaver's head

Amsterdam, DeVries Antique Prints lres 416 Grande

Star Forts

Star Forts are shaped like the Pentagon in the States. There is one in Palmanova, Italy which dates from around i598 (1598) and the map of that Star Fort is beautiful.

Remember that date i598. I didn't say that Amsterdam must have looked exactly like the polygonal city because the first angle that we see of the city is not the only expansive Star Fort. There are at least ninety Star Forts cities in Holland alone.

There is a Star Fort called Cufodden. It is an amazing expansive Star Fort, is it beyond the bounds of possibilities that before the events we're going to discuss now, that Amsterdam had a similar Star Fort?

Mud Flood

What causes a mud flood? A sudden rise in sea level? Could it be something like, as we discussed earlier, a plasma discharge event? Well, the people of antiquity certainly think this.

Watch my YouTube channel and you'll see plenty of images of vajra's which seem to be like plasma discharges. Particularly look out for one/of Sicily in 2i14 BC, and there's also a 2,000 year-old depiction of a sprite discharge. When you look at those, you'll be wondering why you doubted that it is plasma.

Whatever caused the mud floods, the liquefaction by a natural plasma discharge, or liquefaction, using a fasces type technology, seems that it didn't destroy all of pre-flood Amsterdam.

If you take a slice of Palmanova pizza and overlay it on Amsterdam, surprisingly, it pretty much looks the same. So, imagine that something came in and all that was left of the original Palmanova Star Fort system, and what remained was the same scenario as with Amsterdam.

Compare the two maps, one from i598 with a map that was produced 250 years later. It looks like something has taken out a good portion of the city. It looks like the buildings are not there, some of them are there and some of them are not. Every single building seems broken and partially rebuilt. A lot of the pieces of former complete bricks, some of the inner patios have half survived. Everything else outside isn't there. What could cause such destruction? Was it a bombardment?

In the images available, you will also see that the Star Fort walls have survived but that most of the buildings made of brick were partially destroyed, or just disappeared. Some of the Star Fort systems are inactive in those images.

If we compared the Palmanova Star Fort and turned it to the same angle as to where Amsterdam is situated, you would see that the angles for the streets seem to be the same.

There's a 500-year-old (apparent) real map that I have and it shows canals going off in this direction. One shows a perfectly planned layout, but there seem to be no people. I'm wondering if they were trying to rebuild to the original shape to what was there before. It didn't exactly plan out the way they thought it would. To my mind, it looks like they hit that area, completely lost all knowledge and then, just sort of made it into a square. For some reason they altered the original plan of the area, maybe they just needed resources or after events, to improve economically so they could get the city strong enough to get it back on its feet. Who knows? Three straight streets, and three straight corners.

The details I have provided give undeniable proof those are maps of the planning. What you will find is perfect geometry for a Star Fort system. But for some reason something happened, my bet is on a mud flood.

The Amsterdam Concert Hall

The Royal Concert Hall, in Amsterdam, is a Tartarian quality masonry building. It's used for opera and other musical and theatrical performances. The interior is sublime. There is a giant organ and, before you go into the concert, you wait in a fantastic quality infrastructure.

It's the best you could get anywhere in the

world.

The images available for it today are from the i900s, but it was only built in i883. Photography had been around for a long time, but there is no photograph of this construction, not even of the repairs that were done.

There are earlier pictures, one is a painting by H.W. Bianic. i887. The building is depicted in the middle of swampy fields, covered in smelly cow dung with no pavements around it and no roads leading up to it. This giant Tartarian quality building is located where the only piece of estate is an art palace – a classical music concert hall. Only the richest and most educated and the elitist of High Society folk seem to be able to attend. The odd thing is, it's in the middle of a muddy field surrounded by the smell of horse and cow dung. It makes zero sense.

Exterior facade in pasture, 1887

Now, what could have happened? Floods? You may ask, what's he talking about, floods? Well, these floods seemed to have happened in the i700s. It was a big event and all that is left above ground is the biggest and highest quality structures you could find – only the churches and the Tartarian structures survived. This is not the only example we have.

The Rijksmuseum

There's another building, the Rijksmuseum. No paved roads lead up to the building, only grass sand and mud. These buildings were erected for the richest people in Amsterdam. You wouldn't want them to step in the dirt - bet that gave good industry to shoe shiners in those days!

The Paleis van Volksvlijt

There's another one called the Paleis van Volksvlijt, The Palace of the People's Deliverance. This is a Tartarian style building, the same style as the Crystal Palace in London, in i864. It was made almost entirely of glass, stone and iron with little or no wood.

The strange thing about it is that it almost entirely vanished in a fire in i929. Very unusual circumstances. It was in the centre of the city, so it would make sense to have some sort of path leading up to this unbelievable Tartarian structure which was destroyed.

But then what seems to happen to these great buildings is that they are dug out and cleaned, used for 55 years and then demolished. The Paleis van Volksvlijt was made of iron, glass and stone again, just like the Crystal Palace in London. These buildings burned completely in less than 24 hours and left no trace, nothing.

To give you an example, an aeroplane flew over the area the day before and took a photograph of it. Then the day after, the aeroplane flew the same flight path and took another photograph. In the second photograph, it had completely vanished off the face off the earth. Stone and metal, apparently, all burns to dust.

The Heineken beer factory

There are other examples of other things stuck in the mud. The Heineken Beer factory was built in the middle of nowhere, there were no paved roads for deliveries to transport the beer into Amsterdam, so how did the workers get to it?

~+~

So, what we thought was Amsterdam, was destroyed in a mud flood and then it was partially rebuilt. They seem to have reached the ancient buildings, refurbished them and changed the dates of their construction. To avoid a repeat of these floods, they started building stronger, bigger dams.

The Dutch are very smart people, their engineering, even to this day, is mind-blowing.

CONCLUSION

The most advanced thinkers on this plane can be only the ones who are working out how this earthworks. They are the people who have paid attention to history, listened to the questions that have been raised over the centuries and they are the ones who have been persistent in their research, unearthing many clues to humanity's origins.

There are many ways that we can determine how this world works, but most scientists have been closed off to the idea that our ancestors were, at one time in our history, born to believe. Subsequently, those who believe it now are, like our ancestors were, vilified or even 'burned at the stake' for not going with the program.

To unearth the secrets of our history, we must continuously look for clues. Anomalies that present themselves as questions to be answered must be researched. To make any of this research real, we must continue to question, continue to argue our point of view and continue to do it in as intelligent a manner as possible.

Having read through all of the chapters in this book, and watched my YouTube videos, some do think that I'm the crazy one. Well, I believe it's only the crazy people who are willing, or have enough courage, to question the so-called experts. If you have not questioned the notion that humanity has been spoon-fed from birth, then I have to say, you haven't lived, people.

In this book, I've presented a simple step-by-step theory, with images that go to prove beyond a shadow of a doubt, how this reality of ours exists.

In the YouTube videos, you'll find more detailed information that is constantly being unearthed. By watching those, you'll be able to allow your mind to imagine more of what I'm putting forward in these pages.

If you have only just started to figure out that our history is a lie, or have only just begun to question what is happening on a bigger scale, then as you begin your journey I can honestly say that you're in for a mind-blowing adventure, to say the least.

Don't be afraid of what you'll find. Question everything - even me! When you question, you learn. When you learn something new for the first time, it might seem extra-ordinary and too fanciful to be true but let it sit with you for a while. Your mind will begin to move the cogs into place and soon you'll be able to understand.

When you visit my website and look around at the images that have been pulled together by a team of wonderfully enthusiastic people, you'll begin to wonder how on earth this earth could be a globe. But, for now, whether you agree or disagree, the Flat Earth British will continue to uncover new evidence, daily.

Come along for the ride.

APPENDIX

REFERENCES

Many images were sourced by Martin's 'Hive Mind', his research team. You can see more by visiting his YouTube channels Flat Earth British or Martin Liedtke and his website: http://www.flatearthbritish.info/ Some images were sourced from Pixabay.com which were free for commercial use with no attribution required, however, artiste's names are quoted beneath the applicable image.

Each chapter in this book was transcribed and edited from the following YouTube presentations:

CHAPTER 1 THE RESET SYSTEM- Transcript from FLAT EARTH BRITISH, Martin Liedtke, YouTube. Chapter 1 The Ancient 'Fasces' Energy Weapon.

CHAPTER 2 TECHNASMA - Transcript from FLAT EARTH BRITISH, Martin Liedtke, YouTube. Chapter 2 The Greatest Story Never Told.

CHAPTER 3 FASCES - Transcript from FLAT EARTH BRITISH, Martin Liedtke, YouTube. Chapter 3 The Greatest Story Never Told.

CHAPTER 4 THE WEAPON OF CHOICE - Transcript from FLAT EARTH BRITISH, Martin Liedtke, YouTube. Chapter 4 The Greatest Story Never Told.

NOTE: During the time of publishing Martin's book, his channel was hacked, and a lot of his work was lost, re-collected and re-presented. Therefore, the titles of each of these presentations may have slightly changed. To view any of his work, simply visit his YouTube channel and pick a topic relevant to the area of research that interests you.

Look up the website: ResearchGate

ABOUT THE AUTHOR

Martin Liedtke is a proud Welshman who lives in Cardiff. An important advocate for living at one with this realm, Martin, had a fascination for the way humans used to live and found himself working on a variety of archaeological digs. There, after too many questions raised their heads, he preferred not to stick with the narrative being presented and found a way to go about unearthing more of the real history of the world.

His work on YouTube demonstrates he is an avid researcher and disciplined advocate for getting to the root cause of the issues at hand with a tenacity to get to the truth.

Martin presents some highly popular YouTube channels, which you can view on Martin's official website. There you will find thousands of images linked to this book, is on the following site:

http://www.flatearthbritish.info/

MARTIN LIEDTKE'S DAILY MIND-BLOWING RESEARCH VIDEOS ARE EXPOSING THE ELITE'S FAKE GLOBAL HISTORY NARRATIVE

FLAT EARTH BRITISH
Crushing The Shackles of Thousands of Years of Lies

FROM THE PUBLISHER

Every effort has been made to ensure this book is quality piece of work. However, as in every industry, mistakes are made and it is for this reason we are unable to guarantee 100% accuracy. If you do come across any errors, we would appreciate if you could inform us about them directly. Please do help us to present good quality books by contributing your knowledge, email us at admin@bewleybooks.com

Thank you.

www.BewleyBooks.com

Printed in Great Britain
by Amazon

67584939R00119